Every Family's Business

12 Common Sense Questions to Protect Your Wealth

Thomas William Deans, Ph.D.

13th Printing

© 2008, 2009, 2014 Thomas William Deans, Ph.D.

First Edition published 2008, Second Edition published 2009,
Third Edition published 2014

Published and distributed by
Détente Financial Press
PO Box 21123
150 First St.
Orangeville, ON   Canada   L9W 4S7
Tel.: 519-938-2069   Fax: 519-938-5407
Email: sales@ThomasWilliamDeans.com
www.ThomasWilliamDeans.com
Contact us for information on author interviews or speaking engagements.

Library and Archives Canada Cataloguing in Publication
Deans, Thomas William, 1962–
    Every family's business : 12 common sense questions to protect your wealth /
Thomas William Deans, Ph.D.

Includes bibliographical references.
ISBN 978-0-9808910-1-0
    1. Family-owned business enterprises–Management. 2. Family-owned business enterprises–Succession. I. Title.

HD62.25.D43 2008   658'.045   C2007-907109-0

Although the author has exhaustively researched all sources to ensure the accuracy and completeness of the information contained in this book, we assume no responsibility for errors, inaccuracies, omissions or inconsistencies herein. Any slights of people or organizations are unintentional. Readers should use their own judgment and/or consult a financial expert for specific applications to their individual situations.

All characters in this book are fictitious. Any resemblance to actual persons, living or dead, is purely coincidental.

Editor: Donna Dawson
Cover: Sandy Kesteven
Page Composition and Proofreading: Sheila Mahoney
Printed and bound in Canada.

To Jordan and Nathan

Also by Thomas William Deans

Willing Wisdom: 7 Questions Successful Families Ask

Order at www.WillingWisdom.com

Contents

About the Author

Thomas William Deans, Ph.D., is president of Détente Financial Press, which specializes in teaching family business wealth strategies through seminars sponsored by professional and financial service providers.

By combining humor and his experience as president of a family-owned multinational corporation for almost a decade, Tom has shown thousands of people how simple it is for family businesses to successfully generate and protect their hard-earned wealth.

Tom has also worked in banking and in government relations, has been president of a railway, holds patents and has chaired a federal government committee on tax credits. His varied career is reflected in his fresh approach to running a family business.

Three generations of Tom's family have founded, operated and sold their private and publicly traded companies for a combined value exceeding $100 million. This start-and-sell approach, and the annual review of basic questions about the operation of the businesses, has profoundly shaped his unique view of family business.

A much sought after speaker, Tom lives in the Hockley Valley, Ontario, with his wife, Laurie; daughter, Jordan; son, Nathan; and three dogs.

What's New

Every business is a family business, but I was the last to see it.

I believe that anyone who writes a book is trying to convince himself, not his readers, of an idea. In my case, I wrote this book to convince myself that the decision taken by three generations of my family to sell our businesses was the right thing to do, that it has been our secret to accumulating and protecting wealth.

The response to *Every Family's Business* and its unique message has been fascinating. After the book was first published, I was dumbfounded to see it acquire a loyal following among business owners who had no family working in their businesses. The double meaning of the word "business" in the book's title was attracting readers outside my intended audience. I learned through reader feedback that the twelve questions I offer in the book to protect wealth work equally well when asked of key employees who weren't family members. Who knew? It seems that the twelve questions were not only serving the purpose of guiding new conversations within families, but also among key non-related employees and investors, who are often overlooked as potential acquirers of a business.

Through the hundreds of speeches I have given since the book's release, it has gradually become clear that in fact *every* business is a family business. Audiences and readers around the world have reminded me that in the event of the death or incapacitation of the owner, business assets almost always transfer to a surviving spouse and/or children. If your business isn't a traditional family business now, the lesson is that it could become one very quickly.

Whether your business is big or small, close your eyes and ask yourself, **"if something were to happen to me today, who would own and manage my business tomorrow?"** If the answer to that question conjures up a mental picture that is unclear or disturbing, *Every Family's Business* is a must-read for you. It will surely help bring you peace of mind and help you develop a clear plan to protect your wealth, your family and your legacy. This is especially important if you need your business to fund your retirement.

The fundamental messages of the book are that every business must always be for sale and must ultimately be sold, and that making your firm's *longevity* an overriding business objective will destroy wealth with blinding speed. It's a contrarian view that seems right for the times—and right for every business owner looking for common sense help to plan their last and most important deal.

Tom Deans
Hockley Valley

Preface

I have yet to meet a business owner who invited his or her children into the business because he or she disliked them. Family businesses are born out of love—always have been, always will be: the creation of a family business is a powerful and emotional idea. I know—I ran a multimillion-dollar family business for eight years. But only one-third of all family businesses make it to the second generation and less than ten percent of that one-third survive to the third generation. This means that today, if you are a company founder, your grandchildren have about a three percent chance of owning your business. Of the companies making up the Fortune 500 in 1970, a full one-third had vanished just thirteen years later—evidence that size and a good reputation are no guarantee of a legacy.

So what is happening to family businesses big and small? Why do so many simply fold up their tents or go bankrupt? Why do so many owners lack the foresight and wisdom to sell their businesses when they are worth the most? Why do parents pass businesses on to their children when the business is moving toward the end of its life?

I invite you to listen in on a conversation between two people who meet on a plane—John, the founder of a manufacturing company, and William, an insurance executive who worked in his father's business. Both are on their way to Barbados to invest the proceeds from the sale of their businesses. With such a low percentage of family businesses making it to the next generation, our two characters know they were lucky to have sold.

But the similarities between our two businessmen stop there. They have had very different experiences and bring to their conversation different views on family firms. Despite their differences, though, they find common beliefs as they make confessions, debate and quibble over such topics as compensation, relatives in the workplace, stock ownership, succession planning and selling the family business.

Through their discussion it becomes obvious that William and his father were much more successful than John and his family at running their business, timing its sale and cashing in on its full value. The two discover why that was the case, and William reveals his family's secret to success—twelve questions that he and his father asked themselves every year, the same questions that William's grandfather and great-grandfather had shared with their sons working in their family businesses. With this information, the two devise a way of sharing their experiences and helping other families run successful businesses.

The twelve questions are aimed at protecting family wealth from the biggest threat of all—the family itself. Through the questions, William shows John that there is a precondition for his unorthodox approach to family businesses: dynamic family involvement in business requires an honest discussion of performance, compensation and control issues. William explains that if business families do this part right—and do it every year—they will vastly improve their chances of making money, preserving capital and managing risk. William shows that if these discussions are undertaken faithfully and honestly, there is no greater wealth creation machine on this planet than a family business. Love of family and love of a family business generate passion, creativity and a commitment to success that non-family businesses can seldom replicate.

If you are involved in a family business in any way, you are in this book. I hope William and John's conversation helps you build a better business and better financial security for your family for generations to come.

Enjoy your flight.

Tom Deans

Acknowledgments

It took thirty days to write the first draft of a book on a subject I have thought about for thirty-five years; I was able to put my ideas on paper with the help of some special people.

Heartfelt thanks to Jacoline Loewen for her encouragement to keep writing. She is a writer's writer: confident, optimistic, honest and direct—a true inspiration.

My long conversations with Wallace Mark about family businesses shaped many of my conclusions and for this I am grateful.

Without the support of Jonathan Bamberger, Mike Dufton, Glen Fell, Paul Fredricks, Paul Marcus, Randy Schoenfeldt, Mitch Wine and Ted Witzel, this book would not have been possible.

Authentic stories come from the heart. To my editor, Donna Dawson, thank you for bringing clarity and structure to an emotional manuscript—you have a wonderful gift.

To my wife, Laurie; daughter, Jordan; and son, Nathan, thank you for letting me share my story—our story—with families around the world.

And finally, to my parents, thank you for the opportunities you have given me, opportunities that many children working in and outside family businesses are seldom afforded. The greatest honor and experience of my life was working with my father. Your patience and wisdom will always guide me.

1

Confessions on Flight 371

Flight 371 to Barbados was boarding at gate 28. William Cartwright approached the ticket agent and fumbled for his passport; he still wasn't used to presenting his ID at the gate. The ticket agent showed great patience as William checked at least four pockets for his boarding pass and passport. "Enjoy your flight, Mr. Cartwright," she said as she handed William's documents back to him.

As he moved his slender 47-year-old frame down the aisle through first class into coach, he felt smug about his seating choice even though he had just helped sell his father's business for nearly $125 million. Value was important to William and he couldn't wrap his mind around the idea of paying three times more for a first-class ticket. But it was more than that; William also found satisfaction in denying himself things he could easily afford. On the other side of the balance sheet in William's head—the revenue side—he delighted in knowing his family had just sold their firm for thirty percent more than most financial analysts said it was worth.

When he found his seat he sighed with disappointment when he saw that he was seated beside an older man. There were double empty seats all over the plane. Would it have been too much trouble, William wondered, to have assigned him one of those seats? Maybe I shouldn't have been so cheap and sprung for first class after all, he thought.

William decided that if the two empty seats two rows back were still available after takeoff, he'd abandon his neighbor. "Whatever," he shrugged. William seldom borrowed adolescent expressions but "whatever" was such a handy word.

Distinguished and well dressed, William's seatmate looked about the same age as William's father. His crisp attire, silver hair and rough good looks gave him an air of success. The man was sitting in the aisle seat so William excused himself and asked to slip past. When the gentleman stood up to let William through and then sat down again he created a bit of a commotion. He had a presence; perhaps it was more bluster than anything else, William thought. He noticed the man look at him quizzically, look away, then look at him briefly again. Having recently given a business school a charitable gift large enough to receive media attention, William had been recognized in public before. He sensed that perhaps he had just been spotted and tagged.

Something about the look of the man beside him—perhaps his tasteful clothing, elegant watch and expensive-looking briefcase—continued to draw William's attention; something about his body language and mannerisms piqued his interest. William had always trusted his gut—he didn't understand it, but he listened; he even picked stocks on a whim—and his gut was now telling him he should not change seats and that the man beside him was worth talking to.

After he was settled, William began the conversation. "Have you been to Barbados before?" he asked.

"No, it's my first time," replied the gentleman.

"Well, you're going to love it—it's a heck of a place to do business. The banking and investment community is world-renowned."

"Do you have investments in Barbados?" the man asked.

"No, but I'm on my way to meet some investment people now. We just sold the family business and I'm heading down to look at some interesting options."

The man turned to face William more fully. "Well as serendipity would have it, I sold my family business last year and I'm going to Barbados for some investment and tax advice." The two men smiled broadly at the coincidence.

William knew that flights to Barbados were always interesting; the average net worth of each passenger was many times the national average. The island's low corporate tax rates allowed people to invest money and pay only a fraction of the tax they would pay at home. William understood that to be investing in Barbados you needed to be in a certain snack bracket, and after years of hard work, risk taking and luck, William was finally "Barbados rich."

William had learned on previous trips to the island that many young Barbados-rich parents traveled separately, one of them one flight behind the other. This staggered flying was all about managing their risk and ensuring that their children weren't left without both parents if the plane crashed. Managing risk was precisely how William ran his life—and was now the way he managed his wealth.

A flight attendant was impatiently helping an elderly couple two rows ahead stow their luggage. It was sweet to watch the two seniors taking care of each other, bickering gently, unconcerned with those around them; cultivating a public persona had not been part of their duet for decades. The lack of sympathy, care and patience that the flight attendant showed the couple didn't escape William's attention. His deep respect for those older than he had been shaped by his close relationship with the two dominant forces in his life, his father and grandfather.

Turning his attention back to his seatmate and sliding into business mode, William extended his hand and introduced himself. "William Cartwright."

"John Evason," the man replied. "Nice to meet you." The two exchanged business cards. Glancing at William's, John added, "PhD, huh?" William smiled and shrugged modestly. "You seem young to be selling a business. Did you start the firm or were there other family members involved?"

"It was just my father and me."

"Ah, you're lucky," John shot back. "In my business, at the end, there was only my son directly involved too, but like every family business, everyone else was fully involved with their opinions."

William smiled when he heard John's blunt response—he knew exactly what John was referring to.

"I don't know about you." John continued, "but I think family businesses are like the mafia."

"How so?" William asked.

"They only kill their own." John and William both had big loud laughs and everyone nearby looked at them, some disapprovingly.

William said more quietly. "So it seems we have a few things in common. Tell me more about your business—and about working with your son." William didn't ask John what he really wanted to know: whether John's son was still talking to him. John's slight bluster gave William the impression that John might have been tough to work for. Knowing now that John had a son in his business, William would bet that John had a family business story reminiscent of so many others—

acrimonious and bitter. William knew from his own experience that selling a family business was a tough, gut-wrenching process full of emotion and hard work. Nothing tested a family more than selling their businesses, he thought.

Announcements from the captain and the aircraft safety presentation prevented John from answering immediately, but William wanted to pursue what he felt would be an interesting and illuminating conversation. Studying family business had become a bit of an obsession for him of late. He knew, though, that it could be awkward for John. If John's family business was like every other one William knew of, his neighbor likely harbored regret, disappointment and frustration about his business. William wanted to satisfy his curiosity.

Even though he had initiated the conversation with John, William usually had little time for pointless small talk. A good friend had given him a copy of Anthony de Mellow's *Awareness*. The book changed William's view of the world—and changed his approach to business. It had convinced him that everything people said and did advanced their own self-interest. Skeptical at first, William had tested the book's hypothesis and found it to be sound. He even acknowledged to himself that the recent donation he and his father had made had been made out of self-interest: they both simply loved the feeling of giving (though the media attention didn't feel bad either).

The captain now announced that there would be a delay as the plane waited its turn to take off. William sighed. He began to consider what he could get out of his conversation with John—because he knew John was asking himself the same thing. Do I pursue it, William wondered, or do I drop it and get out my spreadsheets? He knew that everyone who sits beside a stranger on a plane goes through this go/no-go thought process. Most don't allow themselves to acknowledge their pursuit of self-interest; others dismiss self-servitude as being beyond their repertoire of motives. Nothing could be further from the truth, William had learned. But William knew he was a connector, someone who approached people like one big exciting social experiment, and his sense of curiosity made him want to talk to this guy.

William never struggled with big decisions; it was the small ones he really grappled with, the little things that eluded his instinct. His decision to engage the stranger beside him seemed oddly like a big decision. It had gone through his gut and come back feeling right.

William took up the conversation again when it was quiet. "What kind of business did you own?"

"We had a furniture manufacturing company with plants in Canada and the US; we had about 260 employees," John told him.

Abandoning caution, William threw out the question he really wanted to ask. "And is your son still talking to you?" He said this with a grin to show that he knew how hard a family business could be on a father–son relationship—and to allow John to laugh it off without answering.

A look akin to relief came over John's face at the question. Sensing that the woman in the adjoining aisle seat was eavesdropping, John lowered his voice. "I really don't think my son is very happy," he said, in an inquiring tone that showed he sought William's insight. "I really thought the time was right to sell. I was getting older. I really had less interest in the business."

"Did you involve your son in the sale process?" asked William.

"No. I was afraid he would quit. I didn't even tell my wife. Michael—our son—had moved his family to join the business and had really thrown himself into it. It wasn't until the deal was virtually sealed that I told everyone what was going on."

"Wow," William said. "That must have been difficult to pull off."

"But how did your father handle the sale of his company?" John asked. "And are you still speaking to him?" he added, turning William's question back on him.

William paused before he answered. He looked out the window as the plane slowly moved along the taxiway. "Before I joined the business my father and I sat down and hashed out a pretty detailed plan. We played 'what if' for several days. What if he dies, what if I die, what if the offices burn down, what if my brother or sister wants to join the business, what if I get divorced, what if we go bankrupt, what if he meddles in the business, what if he thinks I'm useless...things like that. I knew my father had received some advice from his own father, who had founded and controlled a large publicly traded chemical company. It was a unique experience, that meeting, a first in our relationship. I was thirty-seven at the time. I talked to lots of friends who had already joined their parents' businesses and I did a fair amount of reading and was pretty sure I had nailed down all the issues important to me before agreeing to join. I think my father was a little surprised that I came with my own list of questions, comments and concerns that I wanted him to address.

"But it was a bit weird. It felt like a business meeting, yet there he was, sitting across the table from me, the guy who had tied my skates for ten years, the guy who taught me to read. In any business deal I had done before, there was always a degree of anonymity. But in a family business your boss has changed your diaper, he knows you failed math and that you took liquor from his cabinet when you were underage...yet with this full knowledge he is inviting you into his world, he is handing you the keys, not to his car but to his *company*. It's like nothing I can describe. I felt a responsibility. I felt honored. Frankly, I could barely breathe.

"Curiously," William continued, "when I presented my long list of issues to discuss he seemed preoccupied with one thing. He kept coming back to one particular 'what if,' and we discussed it in great detail: we kept coming back to a discussion of all the different scenarios that might lead us to sell the business." William paused for effect. "John, before I worked even one day in my father's business he walked me through twelve questions. This was to be the first of ten such meetings where we sat down together and answered the same questions year after year. Now I had heard of these twelve questions before—I remember my father talking about them with his father. The questions had an almost mythical quality about them because they dated back to my great-grandfather. But I didn't know specifically what they all were.

"Many of the questions, I would soon learn, focused on selling our family business. Sure enough, that day came—and we were prepared. My father and I were mentally prepared, and when the day came we put together a selling strategy that blew our buyer away. We were an unbeatable team. We both knew that if a buyer ever sensed disharmony between us the selling price would drop. We worked together perfectly and we controlled the room. We sold to a large insurance company, but they were nervous because they knew that if the sale didn't go through, we had a management team and a vision to carry us forward at their expense for many years. If things go well in the selling process, a competitor *should* be nervous, because—and at some level, John, you would probably agree—a family business can be incredibly successful at creating wealth."

John nodded his head slowly in agreement but remained silent, deep in thought. Finally he said, "William, you sound like you had a good working relationship with your father. Incidentally, I have to ask. Did you and your father just make a big donation to a business school?"

"We did; you must have seen it in the newspaper. I think I look much poorer in person, don't you?"

John smirked and then looked off down the long centre aisle of the plane as if he needed more time to think about his next question. "Do you have any regrets about selling your family business?"

"I really don't," replied William.

"Well, I must confess I do. I think I really ought to have involved my son more in the sale process. When I got into the last stages of negotiating the deal, the buyer insisted my son stay on for two years."

"That's a pretty standard request," William told him.

"I know that now—but I didn't then. When the buyer kept insisting that Michael's continued involvement was critical to the deal I convinced myself that it was a good thing because I had secured two more years of employment for him. I'll tell you, William, I was simply not prepared for how bitter Michael became after the sale and how anxious he was when he contemplated what he would do next with his life. He flat out told me that he felt betrayed that I sold the business without talking to him first. He kept going on and on about all the extra hours he worked, hours he said he never would have worked had the business not been family owned.

"And you know," John continued, "I had a feeling that selling the business would bring out the best and the worst in my relationship with my son, but I had no idea how much of an impact it would have on my wife—to this day she is a jumble of emotions about it. On the one hand, she was thrilled that after years of watching every penny she spent, she could finally enjoy life without having to worry about money. On the other hand, she knew her son was in crisis and that we were largely responsible. Twenty years earlier she had badgered me unrelentingly to offer Michael a position in the business. She thought it was a good idea...but that was then."

"I know this isn't going to make you feel better," William said, "but I think your experience operating and selling a family business is typical."

"Well, you haven't heard the whole story."

Sensing John's desire to tell all, William apologized. "Sorry for interrupting, John; please continue."

"Well, William, our buyer placed considerable monetary value on Michael staying in the business to help transition it into their hands."

"Ah—a holdback. The same condition was placed on me when we sold."

"But our buyer held back $5 million. And my son, instead of serving the two years we agreed to, lasted only three months and quit, and we forfeited that $5 million of sale proceeds that were being held in escrow." John remained pensive for a moment. "I always used to talk to my kids about how everything in life has a beginning, a middle and an end. I just forgot to mention that that simple philosophy applied to business too, my business in particular." John shook his head with regret. "Why didn't I just acknowledge right up front that the business could eventually be sold when I invited Michael into the tent?"

"I suspect, John, that you really thought your business might go on forever, that your grandchildren and great-grandchildren might go on to grow your creation into something even bigger," William told him quietly. "I suspect that you loved your business, and who but the *person* you loved—your own child—could love it as much as you? When I joined our family business I remember my father saying, 'don't love this business to death.' At the time I had no idea what he was talking about. Now I believe he was telling me not to confuse my love for *this* business with my love of business in general."

The plane had finally taxied to the end of the runway. William loved takeoff, loved being pressed back in his seat as the plane accelerated to 175 miles per hour before leaving the earth. Flying had always made William think in a different way, a bigger way. Big problems always seemed smaller and more distant when he looked out the window and saw little cars traveling on little roads. The trees looked small but the forests looked large. His conversation with John wasn't the first time William had shared his experience working in a family business and he was developing the distinct impression that his own experience was startlingly rare. William hadn't heard much of John's experience—he didn't need too. He could feel John's silence and sadness. William's gut told him that he and his new acquaintance were going to think and talk about the forests today. Never one to be accused of thinking small, William imagined himself helping heal the broken spirits of families in business around the world. Like his donation to the business school, he knew it would feel good to give and be profitable too.

2

Compensating Junior,
or Compensating the VP?

There is always a fine line that nobody wants to cross when sitting beside a stranger on a plane. You don't want to be cold and rude, but you don't want to be too chatty, too interested, too nosey—too opportunistic—either. William felt his conversation with John was different for both of them. Sometimes it's very productive to trade ideas with someone you will likely never see again.

"So William," John began once the plane had leveled off, "tell me more about the business you and your father had."

"He owned an insurance company. I say he owned it— I ran it."

"So you didn't own stock in the business?"

"Yes, I actually was a shareholder too," replied William "a very small shareholder. I mean I'm not that small; you can see I'm about five-foot eleven. I meant the amount of stock I held was small."

John spotted the flight attendant, still scowling, emerging from the galley with the beverage cart. "I can't wait to get a double scotch, though I have to say I'm not looking forward to an encounter with this flight attendant," he said. "It's been a grueling six months; I'm really going to enjoy a good drink or three."

William responded with a simple, "I could use one too," and drifted back into his own thoughts. He reflected on the fact that he and his father had done the impossible; it was over and both were thrilled. More than anything, William relished the thought of using his money to buy the one thing he had never been able to afford before—time. William had the resources to take the time and do what he loved best—think and create. His conversation with John had reinforced the fact that his family's history was sprinkled with business founders and business sellers. The family understood the rhythm of business. William, like his father and grandfather, always viewed himself as something of an iconoclast. If something, anything—an institution or an idea—was well-established, he felt a burning compulsion to find its fault, to tear it down, to strip away its hypocrisy. Perhaps it was this quality that allowed four generations of his family to clearly see the beginning, middle and especially the end of their businesses—before the end found them.

The captain had switched off the seatbelt sign; the flight attendant continued her journey down the aisle. Finally she stopped the cart beside John and took their orders. "Two double scotches and I'm buying this round," said John.

With a couple of sips of liquid courage in him John seemed relieved to be able to talk, to finally tell someone about his relationship with his son and about selling his business. William got the impression that maybe the plane, the anonymity, the process of fleeing at five hundred miles per hour disarmed John and made it feel right for him to confess his trials and tribulations in the family business he had founded. "I've got to tell you," John continued awkwardly as he put his wallet away, "that despite the fact that I've got some money now, I don't know a heck of a lot about managing it. It's like I've spent my entire life *making* money, not *holding* it. The notion of having time...it's new to me."

When William asked his next question, John was open and thoughtful in his response. "So how did you compensate your son when your deal finally closed?" asked William.

After pausing for a moment, John replied, "Let's just say that I felt so guilty about inviting him into the business and then selling it that I wrote him a bigger check than he was probably expecting. As soon as the deal closed I gave him the money."

"So he must be thrilled," William remarked.

"I wish that was so. The problem is he really isn't very well equipped or motivated to get another job after working in a comfortable family business."

"So let me get this straight. You wrote the big check to your son but he isn't happy?"

"The real problem isn't just with Michael, it's with my daughter too. She's livid that Michael, who now has some cash and is driving a great car, is forty-five and basically loafing around. It's a real mess. I involved my kids in the business because I wanted to help them, and the next thing I know I'm the bad guy." John took a long swallow of his drink. "What really drives me crazy is that when we were running the business I didn't really take a lot of money out. Every time we had a great year financially, word would get back to my daughter and she would come knocking, looking for money. She just assumed that I was writing big bonus checks to Michael and figured she was entitled to some too. Truth was, we plowed our profits back into the business, to buy more equipment or build another building to handle our growth. Susan—that's my daughter—had no idea what was really going on at first. The really brutal part was that she would get my wife involved. Her mother would work me over pretty good to make sure I compensated Susan for not having a job in the company."

William smiled. "Let me guess the next part: you flipped some cash to your daughter in the hope of creating family harmony and your son, who had been busting his butt in the business, found out and had a meltdown."

John gave William a look that acknowledged his own bad judgment. He was too tired to be proud. "I guess the real problem," he said, "is trying to figure out where the family starts and ends in a family business."

William asked, "Do you honestly think you can separate the two and have both a high-functioning family *and* business?"

"Every book," John told him, "every seminar, every speaker I have ever heard has stated unequivocally that you need to separate family issues from business issues. I can say now, after having sold the business, that we never achieved that separation. I feel like I failed terribly in that respect. I succeeded financially but mismanaged the family. I'm not entirely certain that separation or even the illusion of separation is possible." John took another sip of his drink and continued. "Really, William, I am of the view that family businesses are programmed to explode; the only question worth asking is when. Anyone who says otherwise is selling something aimed at fixing them."

"It's funny you should say that, John. None of the twelve questions that my father and I asked each other every year was about separating family from business. When I think that those questions were the same ones my great-grandfather reviewed with my grandfather, who reviewed them with my father, it makes sense in relation to the culture they created in each of their businesses. I clearly remember my grandparents hosting parties at their home for their employees; I remember my mother baking cookies for my father to take into the office. Employee turnover was extremely low in both businesses. As business owners, they invited employees into our family and they exported their businesses into the families of their employees—there was reciprocity. It became everyone's family and everyone's business.

"I've done a lot of reading on the subject of family businesses too," William continued, "and it strikes me that when there are so many books written on a subject, maybe everyone is missing the point. Maybe family businesses can't be fixed, or more precisely, shouldn't be fixed. A huge industry has sprouted around the world, from Chicago to Tokyo, from San Francisco to Singapore, aimed at helping families navigate their way through a myriad of issues. I have met people all over the world, in family businesses large and small, from a little diner in Corpus Christi that serves outstanding bacon and eggs to a billion-dollar clothing empire in Milan. They are all struggling with virtually the same issues; some just have more zeros on the balance sheet." William took a minute to appreciate his own prose before continuing.

"Here's a crazy hypothesis: What if trying to fix these family businesses is the worst thing a family could do? What if one of the greatest wealth-destroying strategies is for a family business to be preoccupied with making everyone happy, with getting the business out of the family and the family out of the business and all that stuff you've read? You and I know it's impossible to separate the two. I think families struggle to separate them and when they can't, they feel like they've failed because they've been set up to feel that way. What if the only strategy that really matters is preparing the business to be sold, preparing the family to sell the business and always being mindful that the business is there to make *money*, not to provide family jobs? When I say prepare it to be sold, I don't necessarily mean sell it the next day to a third party. It could just as well be sold to a family member at market value. What I'm saying is that a family business must make every decision with the end in mind, with its sale in mind." William noticed that people were glancing at them and realized that the pitch of his voice had climbed. "I bet," he continued in a lower voice, "that there are even delusional souls who think their business is what brings their family together, that a business is about good business can lead to a better making money family, that the family working close together is the goal and that profit is secondary. I suspect some of these businesses are led by people who are focused on everything *but* crafting a sustainable, profitable company."

"How so?" John asked.

"Look, if some business owner is desperately reading books like *Working and Surviving in a Family Business*, *Fixing Family Inc.* or *Communicating in the Family Firm*, you are probably looking at a family business that is already in spin mode— that's when a business is whirling around so fast that the centrifugal energy forces all the really great employees, value and wealth right out of the business, real clean like your washer does your whites. No book is going to fix that, no book is going to give an owner some recipe for how to bake a happy family business cake. I firmly believe most owners want to fix their family business so they can keep the dream of creating a legacy alive. If a family's dream is to propagate a name, to create some enduring legacy, then they are a lot of things, crazy being at the top of the list. But the family that understands that a business is about making money and that selling their business to preserve capital by redeploying it to spread out their risk—they will be the ones managing their legacy well. Their love of business will trump their love of legacy defined as the business. Ironically, their financial success will be the only thing that produces a legacy, creating happy families that love their businesses. Not to make this too confusing, but this family will also have a family to love because they love making money not making wars. Always hard to feed your family with legacy."

John pondered William's speech for a moment. "Did you just make that up?"

"I have been living in and thinking about family businesses all my life. My father was born into one, I was born into one and so were my children. I have always talked openly to my kids about how tricky a family business can be—and they're barely teenagers. Even my wife pokes fun at my obsession with bringing everything back to the context of a family business. I remember watching *The Lion King* with my children when they were little and explaining that the movie was really about a family business!"

"Are you for real?"

"Seriously, John. Watch that movie again through the eyes of a family business owner; it's hilarious. It's got all the drama and intrigue of every family business ever incorporated. You have the wounded son trying to meet his father's expectations, you have the evil uncle, the distraught mother, the whole preserving the dynasty thing going on. I think before they allow new family businesses to incorporate, the government should make the applicants swear that they have watched that movie at least twice and understand that running a family business without understanding some simple concepts can be a full contact sport."

"I'll confess that if I had to do it all over again I would never have invited my son into my business right out of school. I would have encouraged him to try his hand at anything but the family business first. I often wonder if he agreed to join the business because he felt an obligation to me and his mother or whether he was truly inspired by the thought of making furniture for the rest of his life. I say that sarcastically, William; my son is an accomplished pianist but isn't handy at all—first day on the job he put an upholstery staple through his finger when he went onto the factory floor to look around."

"Oh that's got to hurt. Which finger?"

"The one he showed me just about every day," John said, smiling.

"John, did you say your son joined the business right out of school, that all he knows is the business you just sold?"

"Yes, I guess that's one way of putting it."

"How is he making out after the sale? Is he excited about his next venture, whatever it may be?" William asked.

"Are you kidding? He's set for life and that kind of ticks me off. My father never wrote me a big check at age forty-five. Everything I have I worked for. I have to confess I am more than just a little miffed that after writing Michael that check he quit the business and the new owners grabbed the $5 million holdback. That's five million bucks that would have come to me had he just hung in with the new owners for two easy years."

"You have to stand back and look at the big picture, John. You, like most business founders, placed your child in a senior position. In companies big and small the children are almost always somewhere close to the money, watching the nest egg after the founder has promoted himself to chairman. Even if the founder has decided to remain in the business, children—like your son—typically occupy leadership positions of strategic importance, like in finance, operations or sales. If you're like most founders you didn't want to be the one to stick around after the business was sold. These one-year, two-year holdback clauses are standard but can be deal breakers if the family member that the acquirer selects to stay after the sale refuses to do so and says *adios muchachos* instead." William detected his volume rising again. "What I'm saying is that you were lucky you even got your deal done and that your son agreed to stay. I mean, you lost the $5 mill but you still did the deal."

"I confess, William, I had no idea that Michael would be considered so important by the purchasers or that they would structure the deal that way and put so much of my money on his head…put so much money on our relationship."

"Now don't take this the wrong way," William began, "but I read a great book called *Sell Your Business Your Way*—the author talks about how parents 'infantilize' their kids, never allowing them to be seen as anything but the irresponsible teenager who wrapped the parents' car around a pole."

"I thought infanticide is when parents kill their own young."

"I said 'infantilize,' with an *l* not a *c*. Infanticide—the killing—doesn't take place until after the child has bankrupted the family business, which of course is exactly what the kid will do after being infantilized—viewed and treated like a child for forty-five years."

"Okay, I get it."

"Even when the parent is seventy and the child is forty-five," William went on, "the child president is viewed by the parent as sitting in the corner office with his blankie. Which brings me to the bigger point: acquirers and their lawyers know that there isn't a family business on the planet that doesn't have a parent–child dynamic that with time may be exploited to the buyer's financial advantage. I think what happened with your son leaving the business after the acquisition is common. What I'm saying is, I think it's common for the children to leave money on the table because it's not their money. Moreover, the business has been sold, the legacy is dead, the dream of a multi-generational dynasty is over. What's in it for Junior?

"I would say that if a company has been acquired by a financial buyer, like a private equity firm—you know, rather than a competitor—the chances of the child bolting for the door after the acquisition are greatly reduced. With these types of transactions the new owners will make more of an effort to pay homage to the heritage, values and people that built the company. Junior can have a great future if he or she likes the business. But even with a friendly takeover, the kids may leave the business because they can't adjust to, say, new policies and procedures, like not being permitted to run their personal vacation expenses through the business."

"I guess treating a family business like a drive-through ATM might have worked before, but it usually fails to create that warm Norman Rockwell feeling that a new owner is looking for," John observed.

"You're dead right on that one."

"William, I'm seventy-seven; could you use a different expression?"

"Okay you're bang on. Now, at the other end of the spectrum are strategic buyers—competitors—which we both know will pay a higher price for an acquired business. After the sale the acquirer usually moves very quickly to cut costs—mainly in the form of people—to make the deal work financially for themselves. Nothing in business is more ghoulish or soul-destroying than forcing a child to sit in a ringside seat and watch the dismantling of the family business that he has poured himself into. Humiliating, depressing and psychologically damaging is the only way to describe a child serving a long acrimonious holdback employment agreement. If that child has no economic incentive to stay, they won't. You can bet the farm on it. Or you can plan for it.

"John, can I ask why you didn't hold off writing your happy family check until after your son had completed his two-year contract and the $5 million holdback was in your hands?"

"Michael said that he simply wouldn't serve the time unless I squared up with him. I am not a huge fan of Shakespeare but I do remember uttering 'et tu Brute' when my daughter called with the news that my son had quit only three pathetic months after the acquisition. My consummate underperforming son delivered his ultimate coup de grâce when I least expected it. What a time for him to grow a backbone."

"Remember what I said about infantilizing? Maybe he always had courage," William suggested. "The fact of the matter is that no two families are the same and certainly no two family businesses are the same. Like I said earlier, even with a well-constructed plan, it's tough for a parent and child to get the business relationship perfectly right. I'm not sure you can anticipate everything, but that doesn't mean you shouldn't try."

John slouched and let out a big sigh. He held up his plastic glass. "Here's a toast to the most dysfunctional institution on the planet." Despite the fact that he didn't agree family businesses had to be dysfunctional, William raised his glass out of politeness and tapped it against John's and the two shared a sip and a moment to reflect on what had just been said. The scotch and some straight talk about business were refreshing.

William believed that the self-interest both he and John were pursuing in their conversation had nothing to do with money and everything to do with understanding themselves better. For John it seemed to mean understanding whether all the energy and sacrifice he had poured into his family business were ultimately worth the money he was about to invest in Barbados, and understanding that as family businesses go he had just barely beaten the odds and avoided total financial ruin.

For William the connector, his social experiment was just beginning. He wanted to confirm whether his true talent lay in helping family businesses by sharing the power of the twelve questions that had made his great-grandfather, grandfather and now his father exceedingly wealthy—could William make it four in a row? William knew that whatever he did, the profit from the sale of his great-grandfather's saddle company would be hard at work in his business and accorded the respect that inherited money deserves. The legacy that William would protect and grow was so different than the legacy most people pursue.

3

Exit Strategies:
The Progeny Dilemma

Turbulence woke John from a daydream. The rocking of the plane was so strong that a flight attendant made an announcement asking everyone to return to their seats, fasten their seatbelts and put their chairs in the "up-tight" position. Only William and the couple in front of them laughed. "I just love it when people mangle the English language," he giggled. John, foggy from the scotch, had no idea what William was talking about.

They sat in silence for a while. William knew that he had been direct with John and that John might be feeling more than a little disheartened by some of the mistakes that William's questioning had revealed. William remembered something his grandfather used to say: "When I'm mad, and stop and think about it, I'm usually mad at myself." He hoped John had the wisdom to reflect and to see that any disappointment or anger was rooted in his own shortcomings.

Despite his understanding of John's disappointment, William kept probing John for more answers. "Tell me," he asked him. "Why did you encourage your son to join the business right out of school?" William guessed that like most parents John thought he was providing his son with the opportunity of a lifetime. But William had another theory that he wanted to run by John. "Did you ask him to join the business because it gave you a way out?"

"No, I never viewed it that way at all. I'll tell you why Michael joined the business right out of school. He and his wife were expecting their first child and my loving wife thought it would be a brilliant idea if Michael joined the business and moved closer to us. And I didn't have one of those 'what if' discussions with him, the kind you had with your father, because he was a kid and he was desperate and thankful just to have a job," John explained. "You might think I'm callous for selling the business and turfing my own son out to fend for himself, but it was my business, I started it and it was my life's work. I wanted to sell. There is no simple way of saying it other than to tell you that this whole mess is my wife's fault. Inviting Michael into the business never felt right for me; it felt complicated and emotionally draining for both of us from day one."

John gave William a moment to absorb this information before continuing. "Now I'd like to know what you thought of your father's decision to sell your family's business. Oh," John interrupted himself brightly when he saw the seatbelt sign go out, "before you answer, I could use another drink— and you're buying." Despite John's recent wealth, a lifetime of penny-pinching was deeply embedded in his personality.

"Sounds good; I'll ring for our cheerful flight attendant." The flight attendant arrived moments later wearing what could only be described as her best plastic smile.

"Two more double scotches, please," said William. Without replying, the flight attendant, whose badge revealed that her name was Theresa, gave a bigger smile that both John and William saw turn deadpan just a fraction of a moment sooner than it should have as she spun on her heel to retrieve the drinks. "Remind me to tell you about the time I was on a flight and some drunken guy called a flight attendant 'waitress.' It was hilarious."

John smiled. "Was that drunken guy you?"

"No." William saw that John might not be convinced. "Really!"

After the captain finished announcing that the seatbelt sign had been turned off, John repeated his question. "So what do you think of your father's decision to sell the business?"

"Fantastic," said William. "I work in fives."

"What are fives?"

"Fives are years," William told him. "I have always worked in jobs, or should I say on projects, for three to five years. In fairness, though, when I joined the family business I thought my five-year window thing would pass and I would slide through the rest of my life toiling in the biz and maybe even hand it over to my kids. But John, I got into the business at thirty-seven and sure enough, after three—and certainly after five—years I was done."

"What do you mean 'done'?"

"I was bored; I was in at eight-thirty, home at six, Monday to Friday. I missed the ability to come and go as I pleased. I have never minded working long hours; it was just that I was leading the company and I felt I had to set the tone: if I could come and go as I pleased, why not everybody else? I really felt trapped. I felt an obligation to run the company like my father had. But it wasn't my style to run it that way; it was draining the life right out of me. Every time some interesting job or opportunity came up, I felt an overwhelming frustration that I couldn't just pack up and move because who but me would run the business? Leaving the thing for my father to run again seemed cruel and wrong—especially since he picked me and not my sister or brother to run it. You want to know what I felt in my gut when we sold the business?" William finished. "Fantastic."

"So when your father announced that he wanted to sell you were happy but surprised?"

"No John. Remember our twelve questions? Every year like clockwork my father pulled out the forms with the questions he had received from my grandfather and we would methodically go through each one. Every year he and I could both gauge my engagement—or lack thereof, we could gauge the health of the business and we made a joint decision to sell—it was a collective decision. Because the questions are to be answered by the parent and the child, the process of contrasting the responses to identical questions, and in some case different questions for the parent and child, is what produces the valuable conclusions. The conclusions drive the broad strategy for succession. There are no wrong answers, just greater certainty about the future," William explained.

John sat in silence for a while. "It's really hard for me to grasp how well you and your father managed all this stuff, especially selling the business—as a team."

After a moment's pause William asked John, "Do you think your son's passion for music could have been turned into a career? Did he ever have a passion for some other business? Did he stay out of loyalty to you...loyalty to the family? What's that loyalty worth?" William had become more animated and noticed as he finished that the couple in front of them were listening.

John lowered his head, clearly stung by William's questions. Theresa arrived with the drinks just in time to relieve John from having to answer.

William, sensing John's reluctance, switched gears. "John, you and I both know that there were obvious tax advantages to owning our businesses. But I must admit that after selling I feel great. I sleep like a baby."

"So do I," replied John. "I sleep for an hour, wake up and cry; sleep for an hour, wake up and cry."

"I'm not kidding. I sleep really well now that all my eggs aren't in one basket. When my father and I owned the business, people thought we were successful because we had insurance offices in several countries. The reality is that like so many family business owners we were only paper wealthy. We were one catastrophe away from being wiped out completely. Like so many paper-rich business owners we lived in constant fear of losing virtually all our savings. My father and I went to several personal financial planning seminars when we still owned the company and the first thing we always heard was diversify, diversify, diversify. But we didn't hear one financial planner say, 'William, you have ninety-five percent of your wealth tied up in a business with a father who wants to sell and you don't want to own it—are you nuts? You need to sell a major portion, if not all, of that business.' "

John was nodding enthusiastically. "The first thing I heard from my personal investment advisor after I sold the business was that I needed to diversify. So why was that advice so important to my wealth *outside* the company but not so important to my wealth *inside* the company? It made no sense. When I challenged my investment guy I couldn't believe his response. He started by saying, 'John, you earned an eleven percent return on your invested capital from your business last year; that's pretty respectable.' So I said to him, 'Well,' "—John adopted a sarcastic tone—" 'General Motors earned twelve percent last year; let's take a hundred percent of my sale proceeds and buy that stock.' Only then did he understand the foolishness of the advice he had offered over the years."

"It strikes me, John, that return on invested capital from your family business is only one part of the picture. The biggest part is assessing the level of risk facing a family business and no one, not even a business owner who knows the business better than anyone, can see all the danger all the time. I will bet you that you really got cracking at selling your business

business advisors assume family businesses are not for sale; that the subject is taboo

when it started to wobble...am I right?"

"Well, let me describe it," John said. "Over the course of three years before selling our manufacturing operations we had to deal with new competition from China, we had two major product recalls, we had a government tax audit, we had a massive foreign exchange loss, we endured declining sales and had to reinvent our manufacturing process because of rapidly rising energy costs. Any one of these major forces could have destroyed the business. We were lucky they didn't."

"Our experience was similar," William told him, "except that we began to talk about the possibility of selling after about three years of asking our twelve questions. Every year we could see the answers to the questions leading us closer to exercising the sale option. When we shared these results with our professional advisors, do you think any of them pushed us toward the sale option? None of them—from lawyers to accountants to investment dealers to consultants—would broach the subject of selling the business. With me in the business all the great advice stopped flowing because the professionals assumed that you don't sell family businesses when

Junior is running the show. It may be the single biggest blind spot for both family businesses and their advisors. I suppose as an outsider looking into a business, an advisor doesn't have a clue who owns what. All an advisor sees is a parent and a child and then makes various assumptions without actually knowing who owns what."

"Now that I think back," John sighed, "I should have made sure my financial advisors understood exactly what percentage I owned and what percentage other family members owned. Moreover, I should have had my advisors calculating what percentage of my personal net worth was in the business and what lay outside."

"I think," William said, "the awkwardness that's allowed to simmer in a family business between parents and children simmers equally for professionals advising family businesses. I'm just guessing here, but maybe these professionals feel that asking personal family ownership questions is like showing up for a family dinner without an invitation."

John was nodding again. "Now I know I should have been doing those calculations myself, William, but it would have been helpful to have a professional looking at the level of risk that my investment in my company represented. Ten years ago, if that had happened my advisor would have said, 'Hey John, the risk profile of your business is comparable to a T-Bill but you're yielding eleven percent; keep up the good work.' Five years ago you could see the Chinese invasion beginning. You didn't even have to read the newspaper to see what was going on, all you had to do was go shopping at any mass retailer and try to find something that wasn't made in China. Yet not one advisor pushed the sale option, not one of a long list of professionals who touched the business said, 'John, I think the risk profile of this manufacturing business has changed fundamentally—you don't have a T-Bill yielding eleven percent you have a junk bond yielding eleven percent.

At seventy-two years of age you have ninety-five percent of your personal net worth in junk bonds.' Instead, all my advisors saw you—I'm using you as a prop here—sitting in the corner office and they said, 'Well, there's Junior. I think we'll give the subject of selling the business a wide birth; it's a no-fly zone.'"

"I know exactly what you mean: verboten."

"Right. If I hadn't been able to sell the business," John said, "if I hadn't had another furniture manufacturer come and make a play for my business, I would have been toast. At seventy-six, there was no way I had time to make it back again. When I think back on my thirty-five years in business, I realize I took more risk in the past five than at any other point in my entire career. I'm almost ill thinking about what could have been."

"I see your point, John, but I think your illness has more to do with the in-flight meal we can smell being prepared. I can tell you that my father and I spoke in great detail once a year about the threats to our business—assessing risk was one of the questions I looked forward to answering the most each year. My father always emphasized that assessing risk is a critically important step in ensuring you don't love your business to death. Now, I know you've been beating yourself up over the way things have shaken out with your son after the sale, but let me ask you a question. If holding the vast majority of your wealth inside the company you owned was a bad financial strategy for you, why would holding the vast majority of wealth or debt in your son's hands be any wiser for him if he purchased the stock from you? Even if your exit strategy had been to have your son buy the stock from you, maybe that wasn't the best strategy for him. Maybe he did understand that, which is precisely why he never discussed purchasing your stock with the view to acquiring control."

William realized he needed to lower his voice again. "Think about this, John. Like your son, I could have gone to the bank and personally borrowed money to purchase stock from my father and slowly acquired control. I would have needed to put in place a dividend policy to help service my personal debt, which would have accumulated as I increased my stock holdings. Alternatively, my father and I could have gone to the bank together and asked them to lend money to the company to purchase the stock from my father, effectively trading one dollar of equity for one dollar of debt. In both of these scenarios it would have taken time to acquire control and ultimately all of my father's stock. I don't know how many years that would have taken, but the insurance industry has been changing rapidly. If I had leveraged the business to buy out my father using personal or company debt, I wouldn't be on this flight.

"My father," William went on, "had left massive amounts of retained earnings in the business—it had a huge book value. Can you imagine how long it would have taken to gain control? Do you have any idea how much debt I would have had to take on to gain control? My father would have effectively been betting his entire life's work and savings—his equity in the business—that I would run it well, run it profitably, so that it could continue, year after year, to produce an income stream for him. The most important point here is that one of our twelve questions brought into focus the fact that a threat to the business was a threat to my father's wealth, a threat to my wealth—a threat is a threat is a threat. All the fears about the changes to our industry and the risk to his capital—my capital—would have remained. We determined together that me buying the business from my father was bad business for us both.

"Now having talked to lots of friends in family businesses it seems that most of these businesses have less debt than non-family businesses do. My theory is that family business owners can't bear to have banks run their businesses; they are independent souls so they leave their profits in the business in the form of retained earnings. What the founders don't realize is that they are building their own little house of horror that will explode in the form of a big tax bill when they sell, explode when they die if they don't have insurance or explode when the market and earnings go soft and retained earnings are eroded."

William was rather enjoying this opportunity to give a speech, so he continued. "I think there are two golden rules about family businesses that you can take to the bank, John. One, the longer a founder waits to retire the less likely there will be a stock transfer to the next generation, and two, family businesses with low leverage and high retained earnings are less likely to transfer ownership to the next generation. I think what the accounting industry has learned is that founders who have left their wealth in their companies and have comparatively small retirement estates outside their businesses remain active in their businesses longer. In this situation founders want to stay close to their business to understand the risks to their wealth. My lawyer calls this the 'progeny dilemma.' The more a founder tries to protect their wealth, the faster they destroy it by creating a succession vacuum. We both know that the later in life a founder waits to deal with succession, the shorter the fuse on those bombs we talked about. Increasingly, family members are not sticking around a family business well into their fifties, and the founder is in his seventies, to find out if they're going to run or own the business.

"I know of one family business where the child and parent struck a deal whereby the company took on a good deal of bank debt to purchase the parent's stock. The deal was that the parent would continue to collect a salary until all of his stock was acquired. Funny thing happened: when the company had purchased more than half the parent's stock, control switched to the daughter and she was lying in the weeds."

"What do you mean?" John asked.

"On that fateful day, the child gained control. The child morphed into the parent and the father effectively became the child."

"How so?"

"Well, the daughter started to quiz the father on his hours and his performance and the value he was providing relative to the salary he was drawing. The business was struggling and didn't produce the kind of profits it used to. The stock buy-back plan, instead of lasting three years, lasted eight. The daughter wanted her father to retire so that she could take his salary and apply it to the stock buy-back—she wanted it all to herself. It was payback time for Junior and in a sick twisted way she loved every minute of the drama. The last five years were hell for the father as he waited for his full entitlement from the sale proceeds. At the very time he should have been baking in the sun on some golf course he was distraught, distracted and displeased with how he had mismanaged his most valuable asset. Family gatherings were especially morbid. No one in the family but the two of them knew the details of the deal they had struck. The only thing the relatives knew for sure was that it was best if neither one carved the turkey, that neither one be holding a sharp knife in the presence of the other."

"Unbelievable," said John.

"Believe it. And I bet the daughter probably thought she was struggling to run the business and that she had to deal with stuff her parents never did. I bet she thought she had it so much tougher than her father. Let me tell you something, John. When we were selling our business and I was going through some of my father's files as part of the due diligence, I saw the stuff he dealt with every day. Some of the things were financial, issues that would have made me physically ill. When I looked at the dates on some of the memos I was reading—it was the early 1980s, when I was in college; interest rates on the company's bank debt were *nineteen percent!* I never had to deal with that. I think every kid running a family business thinks they have it tougher than their parents did. I felt terrible shame at that moment. As a kid, I never knew the pressure he was under. As an adult, when I was running the business, I thought I had it tougher."

"Listen, William, we all have regrets, we are imperfect people living in an imperfect world. I say that not to explain away our regrets but to give them context. We make mistakes. Neither of us were saints at work. There are no saints in family businesses, never have been, never will be."

"That's true. And I would add that some of those mistakes are made because making money and making great families are competing forces working in equal and opposite directions. It's a physical law of nature. It's family physics. I'm not saying that family businesses shouldn't exist, I'm saying they should exist for a period of time. There needs to be finality, an endpoint. Show me something that doesn't. As I think about my own family's history I find it extraordinary that over the span of four generations and three businesses not one business has fully transferred its ownership to the next generation. Just like I did, all the previous generations worked in their father's business but each business got sold before ownership was transferred. John, do you suppose that this is what the twelve questions are really accomplishing— getting all of the parents and children in our lineage to work together and voluntarily sell the business when times are good—get out while the getting's good? I mean, who's buying saddles anymore? Who's making chemicals and assuming all the product liabilities? It's not family businesses but vertically integrated multinational behemoths. Is this the raison d'être of our twelve questions?"

"Okay, enough with the speechifying and the twelve questions—what are they?"

"I'm getting there, John. Let's first go back to the actual dollars and cents in that case I just mentioned, the one where it took the daughter eight years to pay her father the amount they agreed to. I think I know what you were trying to say about children buying their parents' stock. When a family business sells the company to a third party, you and I know they can either sell stock or assets. In either case the time horizon for the seller to receive the money is relatively short. The longest I have heard of is five years and that's rare. Two years is more typical and many are less.

"But in that case I told you about—do you realize that with compounded interest at, say, six percent, the father could have sold all his stock or assets to a third party at a staggering..." William dug out his calculator, "...hang on, let me crunch some numbers...for a staggering twenty percent discount, made ten percent more money after tax from that sale, avoided the grief with his daughter and spread out his risk by investing in a host of financial instruments. Exit the business. Mission accomplished, money made, capital preserved. End of story."

"What about Junior?" asked John. "The business was sold."

"What about Junior? Look, business is business. The parent, I mean all parents, should say, 'Look, Junior, I have surveyed the market, I have interested buyers that will purchase stock—better than selling assets—I can get X dollars and I can have my cash in two years. Put a competing offer on the table and I will look at it.'"

"You have something there, William. It's close to working for me but something is still missing. There's still something about the way the father and daughter have left things that isn't sitting right for me in this scenario. I'm sure my own experience is shaping my thoughts."

"Well, while you are deep in thought let me get to the real point about the perils of children buying the stock of their parents' businesses."

"Which is what?"

"Missed opportunities. If I had bought my father's stock, I would never have met you and I have a strange feeling we are going to do something more meaningful in this life than making chairs and selling insurance. I think we could change the world together."

"William did you start drinking before we got on this plane? If you want to change the world you should consider a career in politics." John considered his own comment more carefully. "You actually strike me as a bit of a politician. Ever thought of that?"

"Yes and no," replied William, not even catching his own political answer. "Before I really answer, let me finish. I don't know all the details of your sale, John, but our deal was all cash, no earn-out. Sure, there was some holdback and I had to stay on to help transition the business into their hands, but cash is king. And that cash is about to be invested in Barbados by my father and me, and I can tell you our risks are much better balanced with our rewards. I have every intention of buying some stock in some of those Chinese companies selling furniture in North America that you mentioned. Can you see how we are transitioning from operators to financial investors? Can you see how we can use our knowledge and experience as operators to evaluate lots of investment opportunities and spread our risk across firms and sectors and countries and currencies? Can you see how we are moving into the knowledge economy? Can you see how we are going to provide for our families with our minds instead of our hands?"

"Where the heck were you a few years ago when I could have used this advice?" John muttered under his breath. He addressed William again. "So answer the question—have you ever considered a career in politics?"

"Okay, I confess; I'm a political junky. With my career in insurance officially over I may just test the waters. I have always wanted to enter politics with my own money behind me, with the independence from special interests that it provides. I would love to get elected, run on one, maybe two policies and just stir it up, secure a victory and then get the hell out."

"Still thinking in fives, huh William?" The plane lurched and the seatbelt sign came on again. "Looks like it's going to be a bumpy ride," John said, raising his glass.

4

Relatives in the Business…
Someone Call Security

The next time the captain switched off the seatbelt sign, passengers did a mad scramble to the restroom. The frazzled, exhausted mother with the screaming child four rows ahead gathered her bag and baby for an emergency diaper change. John remarked to William as she passed, "Do you miss those days?"

"Not for a moment," William replied. "I love my fourteen-year-old daughter and twelve-year-old son so much more now that they are responsible for their own underwear."

"The first eighteen years are the hardest."

"Yes," William jumped in, "but the next eighteen are the most expensive." The sound of the crying baby grew muted as the mother managed to get into the tiny lavatory. "I can't believe how quickly they grow up. If I ever start a new business, I would delight in the day my daughter or son says, 'Dad, can I work for you?' I would be going to my twelve questions before they even started on their first day. But I really wonder why so few family businesses make it to the third generation. Perhaps it's because the second generation has had a tough go of it and would simply never put their kids through what they went through with their parent as their boss."

"I have no idea. I'm a founder, remember?"

"Okay, imagine working for your father."

"Do you know, in thirty-five years of running my own business I have never ever thought what it would have been like to work for my own father…isn't that bizarre?"

"It's never too late. Imagine what it would have been like."

"Oh, memories fade, William, I mean all I can really remember is that he was always working and he had a quick temper. He had a sternness about him. Everything was black and white. The thought of working for him is actually terrifying." John's final word faded as if for the first time he had seen in his mind's eye how difficult it was for his son to work for him.

William continued. "John, do you think your daughter would have joined your business if you had asked her?"

"You're assuming I didn't ask her. In fact Susan did join the business and she hated it. Wait, let me qualify that; she liked the work but found working with her brother completely unbearable. It was like they were twelve years old, for God's sake. Every time they interacted it degenerated into something unspeakable. I had to referee everything between them. It was pathetic, exhausting, dysfunctional and ultimately humiliating for both my kids because there was always a winner and a loser every time I had to intervene. I would never have tolerated such dysfunction between two other employees.

"The insanity reached its zenith when the three of us were in a room together. Michael would make a point, like, 'I think we need to invest in a new CNC router.' Susan would respond sarcastically with, 'That's a great idea but why don't we look at our cost of quality report and see if there is some other piece of equipment that could better improve operations, improve productivity, improve quality or help us become a leader in customer satisfaction.' The room would fall silent. Her business judgment and logic were impressive. But she couldn't leave it at that, oh no. She would stare at Michael with her death eyes and say, 'Or we could go with your idea and just continue to run the business pulling numbers and ideas out of our...' " John stopped short of finishing his sentence, remembering there were children within earshot. "I think you can guess the rest—you know, lots of personal insults, lots of wounded egos. I would sit there...it was like an out-of-body experience. I would think, how did I get here? The worst part was when the bickering ended and they would turn to me and say, 'Well, what are you going to do?' Sell the business is what I thought. 'Let's meet tomorrow' is what I said.

"Meetings with the two of them along with other staff were better, but not much better. When my kids started to square off you could see the staff bury their faces in their hands. As time went on you could see Michael and Susan were like little generals, massing their forces on the border, ready for battle. A total stranger could have walked into our meeting room and quickly discerned who was on Susan's side and the few who were for the rather outgunned Michael. The meeting table was a little lopsided. Another awkward moment, another mental photo for the family album."

"Wow," said William. "Sounds like both had the Will to Power. Do you remember Nietzsche's book *Thus Spake Zarathustra?*"

"No, I missed that one, but I once read a book called *Wally's World*, about a bull terrier."

"Keep up John. Nietzsche believed that the greatest power on earth, and the secret to life, was the Will to Power, or the passion to rule, and that the act of destroying and creating something at the same moment was the highest standard of life."

"Okay, Doc, thanks for the philosophy lesson, but I can tell you that there were no high standards in our boardroom. At one point, I had read in one of those 'how to fix a broken family business' books that I should form a family council. What a brilliant idea—I mean, how could everyone getting together outside of work over a meal in a restaurant—no yelling allowed—not be a fabulous idea? I even hired one of those family business counselors to join us. She turned out to be a real flake. She almost made me ill when she implored us at the beginning of dinner to all hold hands and give thanks for our business and for the gift of family. William, if you could have seen the look my daughter shot me, it was priceless. Michael just started to do one of those silent laughs— you know, the one you did in church when you were six, where your shoulders start to shake so bad it looks like you're having convulsions? My wife loved the whole exercise. She later confessed that it touched the Oprah in her. Since when did Oprah stop being a talk show host and become a thing that lives inside you? Anyway, for me the bruschetta was the best part of the evening. The only real takeaway value was when the counselor turned to my wife on our way out of the restaurant and begged her to support her husband because he had some big challenges to deal with. But because the counselor had told me that I needed to support my wife for the same reason I was pretty sure that I had just been hosed for a thousand bucks."

"John, I can honestly say that for the first time in a long time I have nothing to say."

"A friend of mine said that in ten years I would be able to look back at all this stuff and laugh. Well, it's been a year since we sold and nothing feels remotely funny about what took place between my kids."

"So how did things end up between them?"

"She quit. You obviously enjoy history—it was my Waterloo. She was Wellington and I was Napoleon and we both knew it. Our business, our family, would never be the same."

"So when your daughter left the business did the relationship between them improve?" asked William.

"There was nowhere for the relationship to go but up, or so I thought. From that day forward Susan always equated her brother working in the business with him being the favorite child. In a peculiar way I almost respected her more for having the guts to leave the business, but how could I tell her that?"

William couldn't resist asking, "Did your son view her leaving as a triumph or partially as his failure for not helping to sort out the problems between them?"

John rolled his eyes and sighed. "It was the happiest day of his life. I think Susan leaving was the tipping point. It was the moment that changed everything for our family. Up till then the politics of our family business was a source of stress but it didn't shake the very foundation of our family. I missed having my daughter in the business. I was left with my second-string quarterback; Susan knew it, Michael knew it and my employees knew it. Only one person failed to acknowledge what everyone knew to be true. My wife held—how shall I put this delicately—a warped sense of women's role in the workplace. My wife believed that our daughter's first obligation was to stay at home with her children—to 'be there when they needed her most.' Making money and manufacturing was

men's work….you know, dirty, heavy lifting and all that stuff.
Gloria Steinem never met my wife, which is probably fortu-
nate for both of them. After my daughter left the business,
my wife's progressive 1950s *Leave It to Beaver* view of the
world only fanned the flames when the two of them were in
each other's company. The relationship will never be right
again. Like the puppy beaten, it's wrecked—damaged goods.
It was up to me to right the wrong. It would never be perfect,
but I knew that if I sold the thing that was the source of our
family discord, things might improve. But enough talking
about myself, you talk about me for a while," John finished,
trying to lighten the mood.

"If that's the best you've got I think we are going to continue to experience the pall that has settled very recently over
seats 33 A and B on this flight."

John ignored this. "How about you, William? Did you
have any brothers or sisters in the business?"

"No way," William said flatly, trying not to sound superi-
or. "Remember that 'what if' session I had with my father
before I joined the business—the twelve questions? Well, I
was very clear right up front that if I was in, my sister and
brother were out."

"That's a little harsh."

"Actually, I really liked my brother, my sister not so
much, and wanted to keep it that way. Shortly after I joined
the business my brother and sister were both very hurt, but
after they saw me deal with several major business challenges
that almost destroyed the business and me personally, they
both felt delighted about the decision. Nothing like a little
carnage for siblings not involved in the business to feel good
about the concept."

John laughed.

"The first year was especially tough. I had so much to
learn and was struggling to impress everyone—the family,

employees, the bank. I think anytime we had a big family dinner, I must have looked like hell, and they all knew I was going through a self-imposed meat grinder at work. There was this big cloud hanging over those dinners, as if anyone who even mentioned the word 'work' was going to get killed. Even my brother's and sister's kids had been coached to avoid discussion of work. They would be saying things like, 'Hey Uncle William, do you, um, ah, like gardening?' I would clear the dishes from the table and my wife would rendezvous in the kitchen and coach me like a yoga master—you know, encouraging me to breathe from my core and to find my inner child. I would chant 'I will not cry at the table, I will not cry at the table.' It was surreal. I'd go back into the room smiling pretty much like our friendly flight attendant. I'm pretty sure everyone thought I was medicated. After a couple of years I found my own identity and confidence in the business and family dinners returned to their former glory."

William continued, "I know a guy who had a small business who had his wife doing the books, his son doing marketing, his daughter doing sales and two nephews doing a variety of jobs. Because mom saw the numbers she was really the silent boss. How well the kids treated her outside the business determined their compensation. This matriarch had it down cold; she ruled her family kingdom with stealth and subterfuge. The confluence of family and business wasn't a bad thing, it was her greatest thing, because she held all the cards, or so she believed. Unfortunately, as is usually the case in these situations, mom didn't understand the old adage about power corrupting and absolute power corrupting absolutely— she didn't have one question, never mind twelve. The kids and their cousins began to undermine each other so destructively in an attempt to curry favor with the Queen Bee that the business imploded. The company ended up in bankruptcy and the marriage ended in divorce because the husband could no longer endure always being caught in the middle in his family and in his business."

"How do you know so much about that business, William?"

"I bought it for twenty-five cents on the dollar. They had great products, great brands and really modern, up-to-date software. The family war that raged was so well known in the industry that when the business wobbled I took a gamble and made an offer to buy it. My timing was good—I could see how motivated everyone was to bail out on the thing. The family had destroyed its value, thank you very much Mr. and Mrs. Smith."

John said, "I read a story in the newspaper that the big trend now is for families with kids who don't want to work in a family business to hire the kids' spouses."

"Now John you have to know this is the ultimate bomb waiting to explode. I know of two companies where this happened and a divorce ensued. It seems to me that one of two things happens: either the business goes into a free for all or the kid-in-law gets a promotion. The business, its employees and its shareholders pay a steep price. Can you imagine how those businesses run with other siblings in them as well? Think about an ex-son-in-law in a meeting with the ex-father-in-law and the ex-sister-in-law. The conversation might go something like this: 'I think we should look at acquiring a retail store in Miami,' says the ex-son-in-law. The ex-sis says, 'Why Miami? Is that where your new girlfriend lives?' 'Cut it out you two,' says pop. 'I think Miami might be a good location…I didn't know you had a new girlfriend; does my daughter know?' "

William continued, "One of the more interesting family business scenarios is when there is more than one child in the business. Seldom are two children equal in their business savvy or business competence. Typically one child emerges as the natural leader and that child should be the one selected to run the business. The dynamics can get interesting when the more competent child is a female and her sibling is a male, or if the competent child is the younger of the two. Depending on cultural forces at work in the business and the family, parents may decide that being male or the eldest is more important than merit or performance. But whenever promotions, leadership or equity positions are determined by something other than business reasons, a family business devalues itself."

"If my wife had understood this," John interrupted, "we could have saved a lot of bloodletting and a considerable amount of money."

"Whenever this occurs," William continued, "a non-family-owned competitor will drive a stake through the heart of a weak, leaderless family business. Could you imagine someone working at a large company like GE and getting promoted over someone deemed more competent by peers and superiors simply because he was the eldest child in his family? It seems ridiculous. In the real business world, it's survival of the fittest and rewards and promotions are based on merit. I know there's still politics, but it's a different kind. You want to understand why so many family businesses fail in the second generation? Just look at who's running them and who has been shoved aside or held back because of their gender or birth order. Wouldn't you agree that good management is the key to creating wealth in any business? Put a child in a position of authority who lacks the skill, drive or capacity to learn and you have a very nice wealth-destroying strategy in place."

"I know exactly what you mean, William. When a daughter, particularly if she is younger, turns out to be highly capable and begins to outshine an older brother, the family and business are heading for trouble. Having heard my story you know I can now swear to this as an unassailable fact. There's got to be a way to avoid this."

family members need real performance reviews with constructive feedback

William responded, "I have often heard of parents bringing in professional management to run the business or to advise parents on which child is more capable of running it. If the family is managing their affairs properly, the children should be getting feedback on what skills they have, what contribution they have made and the aspects of their performance that require improvement. This feedback is achieved through one of the twelve questions. But an independent third party evaluating two or more siblings' performance is one of the best strategies for preserving wealth in a family business, wouldn't you agree?"

"I would not only agree but I'm kicking myself for not doing just that. I know my daughter was actually more capable of running the business than my son, but my wife had some pretty strong opinions on the subject and I wasn't going there. If I did, I would have paid a very high price and I'm not talking about money. John shot William a look. If I could have blamed a professional—you know, a consultant—for promoting Susan over Michael, I would have been out of the hot seat—and off the couch, which would have been uncomfortable to sleep on."

"Precisely, John! You know there is almost no limit to the combinations of dysfunctions that are alive and well in family businesses. I think the saddest ones are businesses that fall apart when the business fundamentals are good, when the business is growing, churning out profits, and the wheels fall off because the family falls apart. Family disintegrations often come out of left field, with no warning or time to organize the business so that retained earnings and value are not destroyed. I would put family disintegrations in the realm of foreign exchange losses and tornados as major threats that can come out of nowhere and take the roof off a family business."

"I agree—the list of things that can destroy families, and businesses, is endless. And everyone thinks it's just bad things that can destroy families and the businesses they're involved in. How about the family business completely ruined when the son won $5 million in a lottery and quit the next day? Family businesses, regardless of size, typically involve family members in more senior management roles. When something causes a child to leave the business, something good or bad, the business feels the effects in profound ways. Children who inherit serious money from their grandparents, for example, often quit their senior jobs in their parents' businesses and pursue their own dreams."

"John, let's take your last example. Let's just follow the love path in that scenario. First generation loves their child and transfers the business to that child. Second generation loves their child just as much and hires the child to work in the business. First generation, feeling that there truly is no limit to the amount of love that can be dispensed, gives the third generation a large amount of cash, which effectively destroys the third generation's will to work, thereby killing the second generation's business. It happens every day in every country around the world, families killing their businesses with love. When was the last time Exxon, the biggest corporation in the world, made love a criterion for promotions or executive recruitment? When was the last time an analyst at Goldman Sachs issued a report recommending that a company be upgraded to 'buy' from 'hold' because there seemed to be a lot of love in the company?"

"What is it with families these days, William?"

"Hey, don't look at me—I get along great with my father."

"Well, you are in the minority. In a company that I know well the father put a stock redemption plan in place and, over the span of three years, he relinquished control of the business to the eldest of the three sons working in the business. The key to this story is that the father had a valuation done and placed the value of the redeemed stock at the low end of book value. No sooner had the father relinquished all of his stock to the son than Junior went out and actively shopped for a competitor to buy the business. Within six months of his father relinquishing control, the son added thirty-five percent to the value of the stock. The son sold the business for $8.1 million but the father had sold it for $6 million. The father chose book value because he wanted the deal to work for the son who was in control and for the two remaining sons working in the business. After paying down the debt, Junior netted $2.1 million for risking his money for six months. Junior was a sniper and knew all along what his end game was going to be. Now if you ever wanted to relive the excitement of a food fight just like the ones you had in college, you might try to weasel an invite to their next family get-together."

"I hope the son who bought the business was bigger and stronger than the other two, because you just know that it's ultimately going to get settled behind the barn."

"Don't laugh. I wonder how many people are serving time in federal prisons for inflicting bodily harm on a relative in relation to a family business reduced to a donnybrook."

"Parents and children who ask themselves a few key questions every year can certainly keep the lid on some explosive emotions. And if the questions weren't so simple, the destruction of wealth by sibling rivalry in a family business wouldn't be so sad."

5

Fire Me... Please

With a couple of double scotches behind them, both John and William were getting even more introspective. William was aware that at least four people were catching snippets of their conversation. The guy one seat up and to the right of John was doing a terrible job of pretending to read the newspaper. William wondered if he was involved in a family business. If he wasn't, he probably knew someone who was. We all know someone who is, thought William.

Feeling that a unique relationship had begun to develop between him and John, William asked John if he could pose a personal question.

"Sure; fire away."

William paused and finally whispered, "Did you ever want to fire your son?"

John considered this. "I suppose there were many days when I looked at some of the decisions Michael had made and thought, what the hell is he doing?"

"But you let him make the mistakes, right? You didn't second guess him, did you?"

"How would you define 'second guess'?" asked John

"All I'm asking is, did you let him make what you thought were bad decisions or did you exercise your authority and override him?"

"I know where you're going with this, but it was my company and I couldn't just let him ruin something I had started and run myself for 25 years."

"What was your son's response when you questioned his decisions?"

"He seemed okay with it. I actually thought he liked having me there to back him up." John paused like there was more he wanted to say.

Sensing this too, William asked, "But?"

"Well," confessed John, "at a family dinner I once overheard Michael's wife complain that I was a bully at work and that I never gave him the credit he deserved. I took that to mean Michael was unhappy with me overriding him—but he never complained to me about it. I mean, if he had a problem with me he would have said something, right?"

"Are you sure you want me to answer that, John?"

"Absolutely."

"Look, I can't speak for your son, but I think the vast majority of kids bite their tongues out of respect for their parents; it's habitual. They probably defer more than a manager in a non-family business would to their boss. Unfortunately, while the kids are stifling their opinions, the business problems aren't getting fixed. Sometimes a strong difference of opinion is healthy for a business if the points of view can be articulated without personalizing the issue or commenting on the other person's character. I'm sure we would both admit that the needles on our sensitivity meters went crazy when we received even just a mild rebuke from our respective family members in the business."

John raised his hand in the air and murmured, "Guilty."

"You know, John, you never really answered the question: did you ever feel like firing Michael?"

"Almost every day," replied John, sounding defeated by his own answer. "Some days, especially in the last year, I wanted to fire him because of his performance and other days I wanted to fire him to set him free of the business and to end my annus horribilis."

"That sounds mildly painful. What does it mean?"

" 'Year of hell.' I chose to sell the business so that I wouldn't have to make that decision. Nevertheless, I certainly got to the same place after the sale—a son full of anger and regret. As the acquisition looked more and more certain, I realized that I had boxed myself in. I was truly afraid that if I told Michael about the impending sale he would bail out. If he did, I would have a big hole in my management team that I didn't think the buyers would be thrilled with—they thought Michael was key to the operation. So I waited till the last minute, when the deal was sealed, and finally told him; you know the rest. In retrospect I should have asked him to leave the company a year before I sold it and brought along new management. That would have been the smarter decision."

"Look, you can't beat yourself up. I can't imagine how hard it would be to fire your own son," said William.

"I—I think it's nearly impossible," stammered John. "I golf with a friend who had an electronics manufacturing business and he had his son on track to be president. After all sorts of disasters, including lots of personality conflicts with other managers—good managers—who ended up quitting, my friend decided to move his son into an administrative position. My friend wasn't ready to sell the business and figured he could park his son and under-work and overpay him. Well, it became such a joke that productivity plummeted throughout the entire company. The father completely lost credibility when driving cost-cutting measures because everyone could see Junior over in the corner office doing Sudokus all day."

William chuckled. "Sudokus. Really?"

"Yes sir. The father ended up getting so frustrated and angry with his son that instead of firing him he sold his business to a competitor for a fraction of what it was worth. The father just wanted to end the insanity at work and at home."

"I never really thought about it," William said, "but I bet there are all sorts of businesses sold at fire-sale prices for that very reason. Conversely, I wonder how many private equity investors or strategic buyers overpay because they simply misjudge the parent–child relationship. As a buyer you can stare at numbers on a balance sheet all day long and never see what's really going on between the generations. If a buyer detects a breakdown between the parent and child, just watch the multiples drop. The multiples drop not because the buyer is worried about the quality of management left behind after the sale but rather because they know parent and child want a way out—and fast. I think only someone who has worked in a family business can read a room and make a recommendation on the health of a business. We can tell when the child is being beaten down by the parent—figuratively speaking of course—and we can tell when it's a true partnership. It is what it is and in the heat of the moment doing a deal you can't all of a sudden manufacture mutual respect and trust in front of the buyers. Authentic comments during negotiations are what drive deals to successful conclusions, don't you think?"

"No question, William. I guess maybe that's why I did my negotiations in isolation from Michael." John's confession hung in the air.

The timing was apropos for William to reveal a little more about his relationship with his father. "I must say that I didn't have that problem with my father; in fact, quite the opposite. When I joined the family business at thirty-seven, I walked in and my father couldn't wait to hand me the keys. I think he had hung on running it longer than he wanted, so when I arrived he bolted for the door. It was the only time I saw him wear sneakers with a suit. He walked into my office with a bunch of files and said, 'Here you go.' I think his parting words were, 'Don't forget to water my plants.' That was it; he was on the golf course. That was my training. I think our first session with the twelve questions went so well that he turned positively Panglossian."

"What the heck does that mean?"

"He became indomitably optimistic," said William. "Dr. Pangloss was the tutor in Voltaire's *Candide* who, even in the face of life's worst difficulties, believed that 'all is for the best in this best of all possible worlds.' It was actually kind of odd how upbeat my father was. But after leading that insurance company for ten years I finally understood his euphoria; on my last day I found myself running to the parking lot too."

"Anyway," William continued, "things were going great financially at the company for a number of years after I took over and all looked good. What I didn't want to tell my father was that I was terrified of running the thing. I guess I felt like it was mine to blow up. I had run my own business before I joined the family firm but nothing as large and complicated as an insurance company with five hundred employees.

"He was the founder and as you know better than anyone, John, there can only ever be one founder. I think that a child who enters a family business knows that they will always be compared to the old man. It's difficult: drive hard and make changes and you're seen as the ambitious kid who doesn't know what he's doing and has no respect for his father's legacy. Sit back and maintain the status quo and you're lazy and have no ideas of your own. Every day requires mental toughness—emotional toughness—trying to strike the right balance between respecting the company's traditions and driving change. More than anything," William concluded, "it's a huge distraction."

there can only ever be one founder

"But you have panache; you even have a little swagger. Why didn't you just reach down deep for some courage and ask your father for help?" asked John. It was William's time to pause and think about his answer carefully.

"On the first anniversary of my joining the business my father called me into his office, the one he seldom ever used anymore. I could see the tattered edges of the famous questions and I began to feel my heart race. So much had changed in a year. I knew what the questions were and how hard it was going to be to have the conversation. It was the first of many hard conversations. For the first couple of years I approached the questions with apprehension and often massaged my answers to avoid conflict or deeper discussion; I suppose that was my shortcoming. I was eager to show that I was capable of running the show and I felt that asking for help was a sign of weakness. In the end we entered into some pretty stormy weather with the business. Eventually, our annual review of the questions became the day I looked forward to the most because it was the one day I never felt alone in the business. It was the day that issues of control were raised and addressed. I didn't have to worry that he secretly wanted to fire me."

William added, "To this day I can't believe what we went through together in that business. Every year my father gave me feedback on my performance, I talked and he listened and made notes. His respect for me, despite some poor results, was inspirational—I knew we were in it together. The answers to our questions told me where we stood and where we were going. Our focus on success was time tested. After our meeting I always thought about my great-grandfather, whom I had never met, and wondered if he ever imagined that his greatest contribution, his greatest legacy, would fit on a couple of sheets of yellowed paper, pages that helped bring both my father and me to a place, to a decision to sell the business at the very same moment, precisely five years after I joined the company.

"John, our success in negotiating and closing the sale can also be traced back to the twelve questions. The questions reflect the long-accepted truth that buyers demand that someone stay behind after the sale to help transition the business into the new owner's hands. Our questions prepared us for this event and I was truly motivated to play that role.

"And so it was that I agreed to the buyer's demand to stay on for a year, which was a brutal experience and a story for some other time. But let me say this: those questions helped my father and me play the consummate long game, patiently checking off items on our list in the sale process, each supporting and encouraging the other as we inched closer to finalizing the deal. We became so good at the selling game that on closing day there was no champagne—I played baseball that night and he had a nice quiet dinner with friends. Another routine day at the office with both feet firmly planted. He became legitimately cash wealthy that day for the first time in his seventy-two years and it felt satisfying but strangely ordinary for all of us. Capital preserved. Mission accomplished. Quite a team," William concluded.

John didn't seem to know what to say. He fumbled for a response nevertheless. "It's incredible how different your experience was from mine and my son's. I must admit to feeling somewhat confused about my decision to stay so actively involved in the business. I have a nagging feeling that I never let Michael grow through failure. I wonder if I created a soft son, ill-equipped to deal with the cut and thrust of running a tough business. Then there is my daughter and the public spectacle of her quitting.

"Your father and I obviously took very different approaches, William. I know that I wanted the best for my kids and for the business to succeed. I can see now, though, that without the benefit of having a systematic, time-tested approach to managing the tough and volatile issues in a family business I was at a huge disadvantage—and I paid for it terribly. My family paid the highest price: it cost us our mutual trust and respect."

6

Show Me the Stock—
Show Me the Plan

William was starving and even the specter of airline food was getting exciting. William and John watched Theresa roll her food cart closer and closer and dispense her plastic-packaged gourmet fair without humor. John remarked, "She is fast and has good dexterity."

William chuckled. "Only a manufacturing guy would notice the productivity of a flight attendant."

"Chicken or beef?" Theresa inquired as she rolled her cart alongside John.

"Is the chicken free range?" William asked jokingly.

Theresa took the bait. "I'll check with the chef and get back to you." John and William both opted for the beef.

"We have lots in common besides our love of beef," said William with a broad smile. "You are old enough to be my father and your son is roughly the same age as me. And you've got to know ours aren't the only two family businesses with the types of problems we've been talking

family businesses are born out of love

about. And we've only scratched the surface of the really good stuff, like the role of spouses, in-laws, employees, advisors, other shareholders, potential buyers, suppliers…Makes you wonder why family businesses continue to be created at a record pace despite what everyone knows are terribly hard and dysfunctional organizational structures to manage."

"Simple," said John. "Family businesses are a concept born out of love—parents love their kids so they want to provide a unique opportunity for them and want to preserve and transfer wealth from one generation to the next. Now that I've sold our business I can see clearly that these hoped-for transfers of wealth, because of the love and innocence with which they are made, are quixotic, foolish, impractical and naive."

"I think your observation about naivety is right on the money. Despite what everyone knows is going to be a tough relationship, every family with a business thinks they are going to be different, that they are going to beat the odds. This confidence is based on their experience as a family—full of love and trust. What they fail to appreciate is that money and control bring out the best *and* worst in people—especially in family business. The involvement of kids in a business is counter to the rhythm of a family. In most families the children grow up, leave the family home, go to college, get a job, start their own family and in most cases help care for their parents when they are old and need help. Operating a family business with the parents in control and the children working is like forcing the kids to never leave home. Metaphorically, a child working in the family business is still living in the parents' basement. Only when ownership of the business— control of the majority of the company's stock—changes hands will a child finally grow up and move out. I don't know too many forty-five-year-olds who think living in their parents' basement is an attractive life plan."

The two ate in silence for a while before William continued. "I think early on after joining the business there was a brief time when I imagined that my involvement was ill-conceived. But I never truly felt my father had any regrets. It was like he knew that the power of the twelve questions would sort everything out...whatever needed to be done to bring clarity to the business, bring clarity to the relationship, flowed out of our annual Q and A meeting. Whether it was an ownership issue or sorting out a rough patch in our relationship, we knew we had the ultimate tool at our disposal. We didn't have to invent a process, we simply had to follow the same path that two previous generations of our family had followed before us."

"More people need to use that process. William, how many family businesses do you suppose start with the positive notions of love and help, only to tear themselves apart through greed, jealousy, anger, suspicion and the granddaddy of them all, a complete lack of mutual respect and trust?"

"John, if the family businesses that I know are indicative of the state of health of family businesses in general, then the answer is, a lot. I suspect the vast majority of family businesses are in crisis and that the crisis is played out both in the boardroom and at the kitchen table. I bet businesses that look like perfectly functioning companies to employees, to suppliers and to competitors are often broken and rattling down the track out of control."

"I don't know...when I think back I bet more people than I care to admit, especially employees, saw every part of my dysfunction with my son and were just too polite to let either one of us know. Then again, even if I had known, how could I have been sure? I mean, how do we really know what we know?" blurted John.

"Okay now you're talking about epistemology, not family business, and just saying that word gives me a sudden urge to visit the restroom. After they clear away the remnants of this extraordinary culinary experience, could I slip past you?"

They finished their meals and after the flight attendant had taken away their trays, William made his way to the restroom. Ever the conversationalist, within minutes he had heard the life story of the passenger standing in line ahead of him. This habit of talking to everyone he met drove William's kids crazy. A routine trip for coffee could turn into a twenty-minute discussion with a tow truck driver about the effects of caffeine. When William went into the city, he often said good morning to people on elevators—they knew immediately he was from out of town. By the end of the elevator ride he could have total strangers chatting with each other and everyone having a good laugh.

When William returned to his seat he could see by the way John was studying the coffee cup he still held that something heavy was weighing on his new friend. "John—talk to me. You can trust me, I'm a doctor."

John appreciated William's humor as a natural ice breaker. "You know, William, I would say that I had real problems almost from day one dealing with my son. I couldn't talk to him like I could any of my other employees. Even when he accomplished great things I never really wanted to pump him up. I always knew he thought he was underpaid, and the stock—the stock was always on his mind."

"He asked to buy stock?"

"No, but I knew he wanted it," replied John. "But with the stock came control and I was just not prepared to hand that over."

"John, this might be a good time to tell you a little more about my family's twelve questions. What if I told you that the first time we sat down and answered the questions, we started probing the issue of my owning the business—buying the stock. Before taking my first step into the office I clearly understood the roadmap to owning the company and how we would establish a value. Every year when we revisited the questions the issue of control would be waiting there for us to discuss. Some years I looked forward to that question and other years it was the toughest one to answer. It really was an endlessly fascinating process."

"I can tell you that the subject of stock was a big sticking point with Michael. He wanted stock as part of his compensation—you know, he wanted me to give it to him."

"I think you and I know that salary and a bonus plan are the compensation for the work you do every day. Stock is a completely different issue. A couple of the twelve questions really bring this point into focus. I think many kids who work long and hard in a business often get frustrated watching the parents take large sums of money out of the business—and into their wallets. The child sees disequilibrium between their work and stress with that of the parent, and disequilibrium in the money each is receiving from the company. Many children in a family business don't understand that their business isn't egalitarian like their family was when they were growing up—you know, everyone getting the same size steak at the family barbecue. A family business, any business, is hierarchical. The person with the most stock enjoys the control—fairness, the thing that drove the family, is an irrelevant concept in a family business. This more than any other issue is hard for children not to personalize. Children who have enjoyed other careers prior to joining a family business understand this point better than children whose only work experience has been in the family business."

"As the founder and the controlling shareholder," William told John, "you reserved the right to take whatever amount of money you wanted, in whatever fashion, out of the company. The fact that your son worked so hard and took it so seriously was his decision, not yours. Why didn't he ask for a business meeting with you and express his concerns and ask for more money or more stock?"

John gazed into the tiny airline coffee cup and swirled the last swallow of coffee before downing it. "It's as if whenever I had to deal with a business issue involving my son, I allowed the adolescent Michael to show up for the meeting, not the adult. Everything we *didn't* say ended up hurting us, and all that we *did* say was jumbled emotion."

William knew that he was in sensitive territory and tried delicately to make John understand his point. "Your business interactions lacked the precision, form and consistency that are required in a family business to navigate one of the most volatile issues of all—control. Look, John, your son can't have it both ways. He can't say he was underpaid and underappreciated. You told me he was a musician and wasn't handy and that he was not interested in owning a furniture manufacturing company. Maybe your desire to move on and your decision to sell were best for both of you. Maybe the only real lost opportunity was the process you adopted to come to that decision. Maybe, like most business owners, you weren't aware of a way to explore all the tough issues together with your son, as a trusted partner, as a son you obviously care for."

"William, are you sure you're not a clinical psychologist? I must say I'm impressed with your insight and directness. So what you're saying is that maybe a family business *can* work and that selling it at the right time at the right price is the best outcome?"

William picked up John's thought. "And maybe the biggest mistake family businesses make is saying they will never sell because the moment you utter those words, the notion of family is superseding the notion of business, and then the beginning of a bad ending can't be far away—not to mention the destruction of generational wealth faster than anyone can imagine.

"We've covered a lot of ground here, John," William smiled as he continued. "Here we are, one seasoned pro and one relatively young, strikingly handsome entrepreneur family business survivor with lots of experience."

"Do you really think I'm handsome, William?"

"You would be the seasoned guy. I'm assuming we both did okay with the sale of our businesses. What are we going to do with all this great information that's swirling around in our heads? How can we help our friends and their kids still involved in family businesses avoid some of the mistakes we made, or at the very least share our experiences?" William let the thought hang in the air before going on.

"As we said before, John, lots of books have been written about family businesses, books that have addressed investing, financing, strategic planning, tax planning and how to get rich, and here we are, talking about all these subjects without really being aware of it. If the basic issues we've talked about aren't dealt with in a family business, then there won't be anything to invest because the business will be insolvent. So toss those books. There won't be any need for private equity because the only thing 'emerging' will be the debt racked up by distracted owners or managers. There won't be any tax planning required because there won't be any profits to tax, so toss all those books as well. As for the books about getting rich quick with a one, two, three program, toss them too because the only ones getting rich will be the lawyers when the family business goes 'China Syndrome'!"

"China Syndrome?"

"Oh, John, come on, surely you remember the movie *China Syndrome?*" John showed no sign that he did so William kept trying. "Michael Douglas and Jane Fonda? About the nuclear plant? No? Rent it. When a family business goes China Syndrome it doesn't explode, it implodes and quietly melts a big, deep, dark hole in the ground where the business used to be. I'm sure we both know of family businesses that have been leveled in weeks, if not days, and destroyed wealth that had taken decades to build up. It happens every day in this country. Some great family businesses have ended badly and very publicly, but you just know that many smaller and lower-profile family firms disintegrate from the inside out in private, with affected employees and shareholders left gasping at the carnage inflicted on the balance sheet."

John sat up and turned to face William brightly. "Maybe we should put our heads together when we get off this plane and write some of this stuff down. You know, maybe even write a book. We have a lot of themes developing here. We have compensation issues, performance, succession, outside family issues, issues involved in selling the business. We need to think about how we can pull all this stuff together in a way that gives family businesses a tool to steer themselves clear of these problems." John spoke quickly as the idea came together. "We need to give family businesses a new paradigm, a universal principle, a first principle so broadly understood that it will reshape the way families around the world view themselves and operate their businesses—with a view to preserving wealth." John paused and became serious before he continued. "William, how open are you to sharing the wisdom of the twelve questions that your family has used for four generations?"

Pausing to think before answering the question, William reflected on the courage John had shown in his willingness to evaluate himself and to share his shortcomings. William knew immediately that John's idea of writing a book was brilliant, and he also knew that John's participation was essential if the book was to be authentic. There was something inspirational about a man willing to explore the rawness of his relationships and his failures. William knew he could learn much more from John, knew there was more he could glean from a man thirty years his senior who had amassed his own fortune—John was a founder, self-made, well-tested and wise.

"I know I've done a lot of the talking on this flight, John, but it has been very helpful for me. You have helped me organize my thoughts on the subject of family businesses. You have helped me understand just how well things have gone for my family as we founded and then sold three businesses. Most important, you have helped me see that my legacy, my responsibility to my family, my responsibility to my own children, is to now found my own business. I have significant resources at my disposal to pursue the next great thing. It won't be making saddles, it won't be manufacturing chemicals or selling insurance." Now William was as excited as John. "You have led me to the next great thing. John, I do want to share the wisdom of my family's questions. There are literally tens of thousands of family businesses around the world, big and small, that are in crisis. I have the questions they can ask themselves to help remedy their problems."

"If we write a book together," John chuckled, "I have to tell you that I hold some awfully strong opinions."

"So do I," replied William, "but I think we can make this work…you seem to recognize that I'm always right."

The woman sitting in front of them turned her head and giggled, further evidence that she had been taking in their conversation and was thoroughly enjoying it.

"Seriously, William, when I think back, it seems bizarre that my company hired consultants who insisted that we have a marketing plan, a business plan and a tax plan, but I can't remember any of those consultants, or my lawyer or accountant or even the private equity firm interested in investing in our firm, suggesting that we have a family plan."

"John, I implore you, please tell me you aren't suggesting that we develop a simple tool and call it 'The Family Plan'? I was thinking in grander terms, like, as you said, 'The First Principle for Family Businesses.' I was thinking along the lines of the Theory of Gravity, something fundamental, something so utterly universal and unassailable that its inherent simplicity has blinded its beneficiaries from its adoption. I mean honestly, Family Plan is a little lame-o. We need something cheeky and sassy, something fresh. If we give it a French name we can charge more for it when we start consulting. I don't want to beat a dead horse but Family Plan is like vanilla ice cream."

"I love vanilla ice cream," said John.

"That does not surprise me. Listen, John, I think what we are talking about is something really more binding than a plan—it's my family's twelve questions wrapped in a philosophy. How about a Family Blueprint? A document whose principles are respected and understood for their wisdom and permanency, not adjusted to accommodate every new trendy theory."

"I have no idea what you're prattling on about but I like 'blueprint.' It's what you use when you build something of value, whether it's a house or wealth."

"Precisely," exclaimed William. "What I am trying to say is that this Family Blueprint could also lay out a *process* that keeps relationships on track, keeps goals in focus and, most importantly, keeps the family members in the business focused on the goal of selling the business at some point—

selling the business at the highest price to the highest bidder, giving preference to cash and without prejudice to whether the buyer is family or an unrelated third party. The stock of the business must always be understood to be for sale. Sale of the stock takes primacy over any consideration of family employment. And family employment will not alter or distort the value assigned to the stock. This will be our universal principle, John. It must always be so."

"William, you just gave me goose bumps."

William continued his declaration. "It could be a simple document, nothing fancy, that sets the ground rules for parents, children, daughters-in-law, sons-in-law and siblings inside the business. The solution to all the afflictions that plague family businesses that we have talked about lies in the business's creative and controlled

sale of the stock takes primacy over consideration of family employment

destruction—selling the business, something that my family has been doing for generations."

"Did you just hear yourself? You just described your Will to Power thing."

"It's not my thing, John, its Nietzsche's and you are so completely right. We are talking about reshaping family businesses, rewiring them to be sold, to destroy themselves in order to create something of greater relevance and value. We are talking about creating a new, more valuable corporate entity that manages the risks to the wealth it has created by diversifying the investment opportunities it pursues."

"You know this is heresy, don't you? You know that to provide a blueprint that puts selling a business ahead of transferring it into the next generation's hands is radical?"

"Ah, John, we are having two different conversations here. I'm not giving *preference* to a founder selling a business to an outside party, I'm saying the business must always be for sale to the highest bidder. If that bidder happens to be a family member working inside or outside the business that's fantastic—the twelve questions make this point clear."

Not to be outdone, John said, "And the blueprint could make provisions for an outsider, maybe a lawyer or accountant or financial advisor—someone impartial—to ask the questions and facilitate the answers. Because not everyone has the benefit of having the experience of three generations before them asking these questions. With some outside help, the first generation could get rolling with this process. Families would be controlling the clock and controlling their own destiny—they could take the randomness out of their businesses." Getting excited again, John added, "They could breathe life into our principle that every family business must be for sale if it is to avoid devaluation."

After a moment's pause, John blurted, "They could avoid the very thing that my business and legions of other family businesses suffered from."

"Which is what?" asked William.

"I created a Random Family Business, an RFB," answered John. "I worked in a company that spent time and energy responding to events and issues. Completely random events drove our strategy. Instead of our strategy being based on choices, it ended up being a series of chaotic, impulsive responses to largely predictable events. I get the impression that you didn't suffer from this randomness, William, but in our company we always had time to address crises. We never had time to plan and put in place processes or people to prevent the crises from occurring in the first place." John shook his head. "But we are going to fix that, William, and we're going to take your dozen questions and we're going to revolutionize the way family businesses think about themselves. It's time to end the insanity and get parent and child back on the golf course together, celebrating themselves as the greatest wealth creation machine on the planet." Heads around them turned as John's voice rose. He smiled self-consciously at the couple in front of them.

It was John's turn to excuse himself from the conversation and visit the restroom. As John waited in line, to his surprise Theresa, who was working in the galley next to the lavatories, initiated a conversation with him. "It looks like you and your neighbor are having a great flight."

"It's been entertaining," John replied. "Can you believe that after just an hour and a half I have agreed to write a book with a total stranger about a new way to manage family businesses?"

The flight attendant stopped what she was doing and looked at John in surprise. "My father ran a business—he was a contractor. He passed away two years ago. He was seventy-four and there was no family to step into the business, no managers to take his place and no insurance to pay the estate taxes. His business simply shut its doors when he died. You would not believe the chaos, paperwork and despair he left behind for my mother and me to clean up," she said, shaking her head with regret.

"Oh, I absolutely would believe it," John told her. "That's the kind of thing our book hopes to prevent."

William turned his head at the sound of John's voice and saw that he was talking with the flight attendant and was intrigued. When John returned to his seat, William whispered, "So give me the scoop. You weren't trying to sell her a sofa or a couch, were you? Which is it, anyway?"

"They're the same; it just depends where you live. But I've had a profound revelation, William. We need to write this book and write it fast. The flight attendant had noticed we were hitting it off and so I told her about our forthcoming bestseller. And she told me the story of her father dying and leaving a real mess of paperwork and problems from his business for her to clean up, but no insurance."

"You know, John, I have never bought the idea that business owners lack the time to address basic succession planning issues. I think people are motivated by their self-interest, plain and simple. My view is that founders who work in their business and never transfer ownership to family or sell the business actually view *themselves* as the business. The mess left behind may look random but in fact it is quite planned. When a founder like this dies he truly wants his business to die with him. It is the most egregious example of passive-aggressive behavior that a founder can display. It is always sad, tragic and disappointing to see family and employees of these firms pay with their livelihoods for such hubris. Not to be too harsh, but this kind of planning neglect is a disgrace and an insult to surviving family members. Not having insurance and strapping the survivors with the financial stress is some kind of legacy."

"I'll say," John agreed.

"And as a result," William continued, "the vast majority of family businesses are like you said earlier, John: ticking time bombs. We know that only about three percent of them make it to the third generation so either they sell (which we know few of them do), go bankrupt or just shut the doors. But this could be avoided if the first and second generations developed a plan together that basically stated their goals and objectives and stated how the business will be run, and then went about creating and preserving wealth in a controlled and planned way. We just finished renovating our house and when all the subcontractors came in they all wanted a copy of the blueprints. The electrician wanted to know how the house was wired, the plumber wanted to know how it was plumbed...they wanted to know how the house was built and what was and was not possible. I'm certain that all the professionals advising family businesses would like to know how the business is built in order to customize their advice for the business. Imagine a banker coming in and saying, 'I don't think you need a term loan; let's increase your operating line of credit and give you maximum flexibility to pay down your debt. I reviewed your Family Blueprint and I see there's a real possibility you might sell the business. I like that you have identified two competitors interested in buying you. Even if you don't sell, I see you have a well-thought-out succession plan.' "

John picked up the thought. "And imagine a really clever private equity investor coming in and saying, 'I would love to fund you guys, but first I'd like to know what's really going on between you two.' Can you imagine the look on the investor's face when Junior pulls out a copy of the Family Blueprint and the parent proudly walks through all the different scenarios they have anticipated together as a team? Do you think that might shape the investor's opinion about the quality of management in place in the firm?"

"Yes!" William was getting excited again. "Can you imagine an insurance guy asking to see the company's Family Blueprint and in minutes being able to tailor a perfect set of recommendations without wasting anyone's time? Can you imagine the productivity of a parent and child working together in a family business without the distraction of compensation issues, stock ownership concerns and confusion about the role of other family members? And the best part, John: do you have any idea how good the turkey dinners would taste when those lingering business issues are removed from the table because everyone knows and agrees that the business is for sale, always has been, always will be? If we could save one family," William finished, "from the horrors of—what did you call it, RFB—?"

"Yes, random family business."

"—then that would be satisfying work, I mean, what I really like about the idea of a Family Blueprint is that the focus is on all the simple things that no one ever bothers to write down, things like expectations, desires, dreams, skills, results, failures and business goals. The blueprint gets parent and child going through some very basic processes that happen in non-family businesses. These are the things I did every year with my father. It was quite some time before I realized how little of this simple planning other family businesses did. If we agree," continued William, "that it's impossible to take the family out of the business and the business out of the family, then surely there could be no more important challenge than to deliver such a tool. This blueprint will need to focus on all the great things parents and children can accomplish together and to encourage agreement on critical issues to avoid as many of the calamities that can destroy family businesses as possible."

"What we're suggesting is radical," John observed. "We might actually end some family businesses in the process, end them right there on the spot."

"Well, if the end means the sale of an irreparably broken family business at a high selling price, then yes, our Family Blueprint will show families how to do that. Remember that the end of one thing is the beginning of something else, probably something better if indeed parent and child aren't clicking. I guess what I'm saying is that it's better to end a business by selling it with a rational plan than to have a free for all at the dinner table in front of Uncle Bill and Aunt Mary—or worse, on the front page of the newspaper when the firm goes bankrupt."

"You know," John said, "lawyers won't be happy with our Family Blueprint concept. I mean, without feuding families how will they feed *their* families?"

"Quite the contrary, actually," William told him. "My lawyer complains all the time about how frustrating it is to deal with family businesses. I bet there are other professionals—like those in the life insurance industry—who see a parent dying at his desk and the kids losing the business because they can't pay the estate taxes. I bet the accounting industry sees businesses all the time that refuse to implement solid tax plans because something is going on between the parent and child. I bet the accountants have no idea why the owners aren't implementing the solutions the accountant suggests."

"You're right. I had one life insurance guy come in and talk to me about his stuff, but he had no clue what was going on in the business. He was oblivious to the fact that I really just wanted to sell it. I'm certain that if he had just asked I would have told him. If I had told him, he would have educated me on the fact that sometimes it takes years to sell a business—and it did—and that in the meantime I ought to put some coverage in place. If I'd died before selling the business and didn't have insurance, my wife would have killed me."

"Have another drink, John; you're actually getting funny."

John continued, "My lawyer was another one who was oblivious to the dynamics in our business. She had a boiler-plate shareholder agreement and seemed unbelievably ill-equipped to draft provisions that spoke specifically to our family's situation. It really wasn't her fault because we didn't, and couldn't, provide her with a simple document showing her how the business was built; we were missing a simple roadmap showing her where we wanted to take the business together. Telling our lawyer when and to whom we wanted to sell would have been hugely beneficial to her and ultimately to us as the client."

"And if there is one industry," William interrupted, "that is well positioned to help family businesses create wealth it's the accounting profession. Just because assets equal liabilities plus owner's equity doesn't mean that they should ignore the impact a feuding parent and child have on a balance sheet. Accountants struggle to provide relevant advice, tax advice especially, that can help second-generation businesses prepare for one of four major outcomes: a sale, a succession, voluntary closure or bankruptcy. If accountants were told which path a family business was heading down, they could deliver so much more value to their clients."

"I know who the real losers are...you and me," said John. "After selling the business my son and I sat down with our accountant to go over the tax implications of the sale. A couple of times the accountant said, 'Had we known that you were going to sell we would had done this or that differently.' Michael and I just sat there looking at each other as if we knew what the other was thinking. We could have saved hundreds of thousands of dollars in tax if we had taken five minutes and talked openly about the possibility of selling the business and preparing our structure for that day. In a company in which we would gnash our teeth to save $5,000 by switching to a new supplier, we left massive amounts of cash sitting on the table for our friends in the tax collection department."

"I'm sure if you asked nicely they will give it back," laughed William.

"I did ask. Why do you think I'm flying to Barbados? So what the heck is it, William, that prevents families from talking openly about the future of their businesses, among themselves and with their advisors?"

"Simple," William told him. "It's taboo. Mention the word 'sale' and you're talking about selling the family, not selling the family business. Remember, business is all about money and I think everyone, families especially, struggles with talking about money. I think talking about sex with

Aunt Mabel might actually be easier—at least you can joke about sex."

With that, the captain announced that they were beginning their approach to Grantley Adams International Airport. William looked out the window and saw the crystal blue water and the pure white beaches of Barbados: paradise. William felt he had earned this trip, earned every penny of his share of the proceeds from the sale of the business. He had earned enough to provide for his family, enough to finally move his investments offshore, enough to start his own business, which maybe his daughter or son would join one day. William was happy but he wanted more, and the guy sitting beside him was going to help him get it.

John seemed to read his mind. "William, when we get settled in Barbados and you have time—and you're not too exhausted from investing your millions—let's have dinner. I think we're on to something here. It's something so shockingly simple that I'm starting to blush. Are you interested?"

William replied, "I'm forty-seven, unemployed, have plenty of cash and am looking for my next big thing. Bring it on, baby."

"Don't call me 'baby,' kiddo."

"Okay, pops."

7

Selling the Business: Creative Destruction

They landed in Barbados. Unlike take-off, the jolt of the wheels meeting the concrete was a disappointing reminder that the plane—and William's idealism—were back to earth. The plane slowly taxied to the terminal. William couldn't remember a flight passing so quickly—he couldn't ever remember wanting a flight not to end. The Jetway extended to meet the plane and as the aircraft's doors opened, a rush of warm tropical air filled the cabin.

The humid air brought the reason for his trip to the front of William's mind. The stress of selling the business and now having to make decisions about investing the proceeds suddenly seemed overwhelming. Despite being tired, William was invigorated by his lengthy conversation with John and the ideas and possibilities they had explored. He was feeling the deep satisfaction that comes from struggling with issues and resolving them. As he gathered his belongings, William smiled as he thought about how a simple saddle maker, whose twelve questions drafted more than a hundred years earlier, was going to have a lasting influence on families involved in businesses ranging from computer software to manufacturing to plumbing. The issues are always the same, he thought, whether that firm is located in Australia, France or Brazil. In a big business or a small one, family emotions and dynamics will be forever universal.

William knew Barbados well, having vacationed there several times. He said to John as they waited to leave the plane, "How about I meet you at your hotel for dinner. Let's plan for seven o'clock, because first, we've earned our naps." William relished the thought of indulging in the one thing that was impossible to do at home with two busy kids and a dog.

"That suits me perfectly," John agreed. "I had planned on napping during the flight!"

The two disembarked from the plane and walked to the luggage claim area. They walked with the older couple who had been sitting a couple of rows ahead of them on the flight and discovered that the pair was in the process of selling their gas station to their son and daughter.

When they'd collected their bags, William and John exchanged hotel information and shook hands.

As William drove to his hotel he began to formulate precisely how they would word the Family Blueprint that would include his family's twelve questions. He had run a large company and wanted to impress John with his ideas on how to save family businesses from the ravages of planning neglect. William wanted to articulate a better method of preparing every family business, regardless of size, to keep the option of selling open. He kept wondering why families wait for their businesses to fail. Why wouldn't they take control of the process, why wouldn't they control the clock, cultivate potential buyers, clean up the balance sheet, time the market and sell at the top—and do all of that with parent and child driving the process together with enthusiasm and trust? Everything that William and his father, and his father's father, had done had been achieved with relative ease and with little acrimony—so easy, yet so seldom done.

William again dug deep into his consciousness to answer the fundamental question of why businesses fail to make it to the third generation. What was really going on in the second generation of a business that was destroying value, relationships and for many the entire business itself? William came up with two theories.

He theorized that in many cases, the company's technology was antiquated, its brands were tired—it had lost its edge, its competitive advantage. He imagined that such a firm's competitors were much bigger and better capitalized. William had a gut feeling that with rapid globalization, many family businesses were simply ill-equipped to compete, perhaps because families want to be close together, not spread out across the globe like a multinational corporation.

William believed, secondly, that quite often, Gen III, as he called them, didn't move into the family business because Gen II loved their kids too much to put them through the same grinding issues they had endured. Instead of looking for solutions to avoid those problems, Gen II simply let the business die.

William knew that the Family Blueprint would need to provide risk and reward to parent and child equally if it was to be compelling enough for them to pursue. He also agreed with John that it would be easier if a third party requested that those involved in the business complete the blueprint—this would take all the parent–child awkwardness out of play. William imagined how difficult it would have been for him to present the concept of a Family Blueprint to his father: when a child joins a family business, the parent holds all the cards; it is the parents with the money and it is the parents offering the opportunity. As time passes, though, the child becomes more important to the business, eventually central to its success, and the pendulum swings the other way; the child holds the reins of wealth generation and wealth preservation, making it awkward for the parent to suggest anything like creating a blueprint.

Thinking about this swing of power made William think about the irony of how a parent who abuses power early in the business relationship usually pays a much higher price down the road when Junior is unhappy. In one of the worst cases William could remember in his industry, a wounded son so utterly exploited by his parents simply resigned and started an insurance business of his own. The son wasn't satisfied with just leaving; he made it his blinding mission to eviscerate his parents' business. Only when their business was completely destroyed did the son believe that his parents would acknowledge his ability to run an insurance company. It was his parents' approval, not money, that was missing from their relationship. William thought how utterly preventable this sad scenario was.

William knew from his own experience that it is common for kids to drive a family business hard to beat their parents' record for sales growth or margin growth. It's no wonder, he thought, that private equity firms love to invest in family businesses; under the right circumstances, hell hath no fury like a child bent on beating the parents' balance sheet performance—and the child usually does. The real problems usually occur when Junior is successful and wants to be paid accordingly. It's kind of like the first time a son beats his father in golf; it's bittersweet for dad to hand over the twenty bucks that was riding on the game. The moment a child either produces better financial results than the parent or earns more money through pay for performance, something in the relationship changes. William felt the twelve questions would capture this as a defining moment and trigger the discussion around the subject of succession or sale of the business.

William knew that the founders in his family—his father, his grandfather and his great-grandfather—were smart people who understood that a business is about making money—first and foremost for *them*. William knew that business owners who didn't acknowledge this fact were probably deluding themselves with visions of legacies and multigenerational empires. Instinctively William had always followed the cash; the pursuit of legacies and dynasties were fool's gold. He felt he was about to reveal this secret, his family's secret, Nietzsche's secret, to family businesses around the world.

William arrived at his hotel and checked in. He took a few minutes to appreciate the view of the beach, the ocean and the sky before he lay down for his nap. As he sunk into bed he thought about Stephen Covey's book *Seven Habits of Highly Effective People*. As with many books, William remembered one thing most clearly, in this case, "start at the end." The end for his family business was its sale. He once again felt a wave of satisfaction.

William reflected on John's belief that everything has a beginning, a middle and an end. We chose our ending, he thought. We wrote the last chapter together, Dad and I. Just maybe the end of our family business feels good because it was our plan to sell it. We controlled the end and controlling an outcome feels good. We sold the business and a new beginning emerged, a new creation, new possibilities for investment. Our lack of desire to rule an old company has been replaced with a burning desire to rule something yet to be invented: creative destruction trumping the benign, wealth-destroying idea of family legacy. So many people in so many family businesses simply refuse to talk openly about selling and when difficult times come, as they inevitably do, family members are ill-prepared and everything unravels—fast. Why don't families start at the end, he wondered. Why do they deny that their product has a shelf life, that their careers have a beginning, a middle and an end? Why does everyone think they are going to be healthier and live longer than they actually do? Why do they wait for life to happen to them as opposed to preparing and planning for the most predicable events imaginable, like aging and death?

William's last thought before he drifted into sleep was of the couple from the plane who were selling their gas station to their son and daughter. William wondered whether, with advances in fuel cells and other new technologies, the couple imagined that many fewer gas stations may exist in ten years. The gift to their children—selling the business on the family payment plan, with the kids making payments over time— could destroy the equity in the business, could destroy their children's careers and tear the family apart if the business becomes antiquated and fails. All the love that went with the gift may be replaced with regret and hostility ten years from now, when no one can remember why anyone did what they did. Not exactly the legacy mom and dad were hoping for and not the lottery the kids thought they won. Market forces can devour families blinded by love. But maybe I'm wrong, William thought. Maybe in twenty years there will be more need and demand for gas stations than ever before; the fact is, no one knows. The only thing that matters is whether that couple has the foresight to discuss with their children the possibility of selling the business to someone else if market conditions change. Anything less could destroy value in the business, and the family along with it. William knew that his twelve questions could protect this family from itself.

When William woke John a couple of hours later with his phone call, William could hear John fumbling with the phone before he spoke.

"Hello," John finally said, disoriented and groggy.

"Siesta is over, Johnny. I have cracked the nut and I know exactly how we are going to save family businesses from themselves. I'll meet you in the lobby of your hotel at seven. I have already made reservations at the hotel restaurant. Bring a pad of paper; we're going start our book tonight."

"Ah, okay." John was still getting his bearings.

"By the way, I already have a title for our book. I wanted something positive that would remind families why they grind through all the issues and hard work and long hours and risk."

"What did you come up with?"

"I was sitting in my hotel room," William explained, "looking out at the beach, and thought how for years I've heard about guys selling their businesses and becoming 'Barbados rich.' It sounded like a plateau, a level of wealth that few achieved. It struck me that I had finally made it. John, without the stress of running that business and potentially losing everything, losing my wealth, I can finally breathe. I can finally focus on small things like the scent of the ocean and the melody of the waves making sand from corral. We both made it, didn't we John? If we are successful with our book, we will help families breathe and mend. Every day I felt like I was gambling everything I worked to create. The harder I worked, the faster changes to the business seemed to come—new technology, new competitors, lower pricing, lower margins, obnoxious government regulators, employee issues…the wall of adversity seemed insurmountable. It felt like someone kept moving the finish line. I realized that the closer I got to crystallizing my wealth from the business, the more distant and unattainable and unavailable the cash was. I know our book will be a success if we can give every family business around the world a simple tool that captures exactly what we talked about today on the plane."

"That's a nice story, but what are we calling the book?"

"We'll call it *Every Family's Business: 12 Common Sense Questions to Protect Your Wealth*."

"You really are a literary genius," John told him. "I love it. I'll see you at seven. And since you're feeling so Barbados rich you can buy dinner."

When they met later, William shook John's hand firmly. "Good to see you, John." As they clasped hands, William looked into John's eyes as if to take the measure of the man he was about to invest considerable time in. William felt the connection and confirmed the immediate trust he had felt on the plane.

As they walked toward the restaurant, William noticed John's stylish suit and impeccably coordinated shirt and tie. "You clean up good," he said approvingly.

"Thanks. My wife picks my clothes—she even coordinates my outfits by putting little numbers on the labels of everything, if you can believe it. I'm color blind," John explained, "so the alternative is dressing like a clown. Luckily she's got a great sense of style!"

"I prefer casual, as you can see," William said, spinning around to show off his wrinkled golf shirt and khakis. His dark-rimmed glasses gave him an educated look, though, which William relished. Being viewed as smart was more important to William than being viewed as wealthy. People often underestimated William based on the way he dressed or the beater of a car he drove. William never let his possessions run his life.

Having been seated by the head waiter, the two felt refreshed and ready to dive back into their conversation right where they left off. John began. "Let's get down to business. Let's start at the end of our book, William."

"You mean write the book like *Time's Arrow*, where Martin Amis asked his readers to start with the end of the story and read backward through time?"

"Guess I missed that book too," John replied. "I just meant, let's write the book backward from its end to its beginning. Our readers are normal people running family businesses and will want to read it front to back."

"Okay. I see as a successful end to our book churning out happy families sitting around the dinner table eating turkey with kids involved in the business, kids outside the business, spouses of kids involved in the businesses, and mom and dad as the founders of the business. I see every combination of family members involved or not involved in the business enjoying their holiday celebration. There is even lots of discussion about the business because there is no jealousy or stress because the entire family understands that all the big flammable issues have been discussed and resolved. Even if there are new simmering issues, our family knows that the time-tested twelve questions will foster a resolution at least once a year." William paused to let John absorb this sunny scene. "By the way, in my ending, John, you are wearing a nice warm sweater—you know, the ones with the leather patches on the elbows? And you're smoking pipe. Is that working for you?"

John looked at William quizzically. "I'm trying to figure out if you were drinking on your own this afternoon. At any rate, what you just described is a tall order but a good start. Incidentally, can I ask why families are always eating turkey in your examples?"

"I love turkey."

The waiter had just approached the table and overheard William's reference to turkey. "I am afraid, sir, that we do not have turkey on the menu but I can recommend the fresh grilled tuna. But can I first offer you a drink from the bar, or would you like to see the wine list?"

William, still smirking, said, "I don't know about you but whenever I'm in the Caribbean I must have a piña colada—but I don't want to hear any girly-man jokes, alright?"

John turned to the waiter. "And could you pop one of those nice little umbrellas in it for him?"

The waiter played along. "Very good, sir," he said, dead serious, bowing slightly. "And for you?"

"I'll have a vodka and tonic."

William continued. "In our family business, everyone talked openly about its sale. When times were good and when times were bad, everyone knew that its sale to somebody—to a family member, to an outside party—was a certainty. Everyone knew that there were no family discounts on stock; there was no jealously. The twelve questions were legendary in our family; they have taken on a life of their own."

"So," John summarized, "in every family business, everyone in and outside the business understands that the business is always for sale...always."

"You bet," William replied. "I see the principals in the business, and their families, fully understanding their upside if the business is sold and their liabilities if the business fails. The concept of providing lifelong employment for Generation II and Generation III is removed from the table if everyone understands from the beginning what their economic benefit is from the business if it is sold and what their loss is if it fails. Everyone in the family—spouses, siblings, parents, cousins—must understand that the fundamental role of the business is to make money and to maximize shareholder value. The family business must be understood in those terms and not as some kind of social welfare agency for distributing funds in perpetuity, even if that's what it has done in the past. If we can write a convincing book we will show family businesses that our twelve questions are designed to align the interests of the business with the interests of *all* family members. The success of the business will spell success for the family. Everyone's pulling in the same direction."

John interrupted, "So if the controlling shareholder, typically the founder, wants to distribute wealth to non-active family members, he or she should issue a dividend to all shareholders and then give out money from that dividend. The founder can do what they wish with the money when it's out of the business and in private hands, including their own."

"Yes, precisely. Writing checks from a family business to family members as gifts is just about the most wealth-destroying seed a family can plant."

"I am a little confused about something, though," John said. "Why do you think your family members are going to be thrilled that their company is going to be sold?"

"I'm not surprised you're confused by that. Halfway through completing the questions the first time I thought the same thing, but then came a couple of questions that made sense of it all. I could see my great-grandfather's thought process. He really was a genius." William sipped his water as if preparing to give a speech. "You see, John, if the founder of the business doesn't provide enough economic incentive for a child to drive the sale option, the sale will never be pursued seriously. If the parent doesn't lay out an exciting economic plan for a child in the event of a sale, the child may well pursue another business when he or she truly understands that the sale option is real. If the child quits because there isn't enough benefit if the business is sold, the parent risks losing one of the business's greatest assets for delivering increased value both as an operating business and from its sale—the child is key."

"I now know that from personal experience," replied John. "I would have paid big bucks for your questions and you haven't even told me what they all are. I didn't discuss my son's economic benefit in the event of a sale and consequently I couldn't involve him in the sale process the way your father involved you. That lack of trust cost both Michael and me money. If I had been more up front with him I might have said, 'Look, the deal is almost certainly going to involve a holdback and earn-out of, say, $5 million contingent on you staying after the sale. If you agree to stay and help with a smooth transition, I will give you $2.5 million of the holdback when you fulfill that condition.' I could have put $2.5 million more in my pocket and $2.5 million more in Michael's pocket. Instead I put $5 million in the buyer's pocket. That was not a good ending to our story."

"$2.5 million...is it too late for you to adopt me?"

"Don't break my concentration, William, I'm on a roll." John returned to his train of thought. "What we're saying is that our twelve questions will deliver a great conclusion, an ending that will see the children involved in a business *and* the parents celebrating the sale of the business with equal pride and satisfaction."

"Yes, and that's exactly how I view the sale of my family business. Don't forget, it's good for the family outside the business to understand that the family working in the business is always probing the market for an opportunity to crystallize generational wealth at its peak—for everyone's benefit. Now, my next point is key: I think full value can be derived from selling a business only when potential buyers see a competent adult child driving the sale process in the name of shareholder value. When strategic buyers are looking at a business and see a confident executive—the child—along with the founder driving the sale on its economic merits while at the same time displaying confidence in the business to grow its market share at the acquirer's expense if the deal doesn't go through, a higher price will almost certainly follow. When a child takes a proactive leadership role in the sale of a family business it confuses the hell out of the acquirer. And in any negotiation I've been involved in, if you have the other party confused, you have gained the upper hand," William finished with finality. "You see, what the questions do for children is teach them to take the emotion out of the business—and note that I said emotion, not passion."

John was nodding enthusiastically so William continued. "When Junior displays confidence in the negotiating room, the acquirer gets a glimpse of the quality of the leadership of the corporation. Our questions allowed me to lead boldly and to focus on the business, not dream about intangibles like preserving the family legacy."

John summarized. "So instead of children working in a family business being upset that their parents may sell, the kids can participate in a positive way and earn money to carry them through to their next great venture."

"Exactly. Preserving the wealth accumulated in a family business must be the first priority for everyone. You will see in the questions that make up our Family Blueprint that these compensation plans can be drafted well in advance of any discussion with a potential buyer. In fact, they should take place before the children even join the business. But it's never too late to get these issues hammered out to get the kids as fired up about the option of selling as the parents are.

"We want to help family businesses avoid an ending in which parents refuse to imagine selling the business because they are in love with the idea of their business surviving for generations—and it slides into bankruptcy. Under bankruptcy the parents lose their wealth and the kids lose their employment and their inheritance. Ask any parent who has watched their family business fail whether they should have

sold and every one will nod their head approvingly with regret." William caught himself and paused. "Did that make
sense? Can you nod your head approvingly with regret?"

"I know what you meant."

Their drinks arrived, William's piña colada bearing a pink
umbrella. "Isn't that cute," John told him. "You know you'd
never make it at the American Furniture Manufacturers As-
sociation convention." William laughed. He knew he looked
ridiculous but he loved being the center of attention.

John got back to business. "William, while you're playing
with your umbrella take some notes because I think I have
another great point for our book. If a family business is always understood by parent and
child to be for sale, why
wouldn't we include in our
Family Blueprint a provision
for the children to purchase the
stock themselves? Think about
it: if the children are adding as
much value as they think they are, if they're as under-
compensated as they think they are and if they think the parents are taking too much money out of the business, why not
have a provision for the kids to acquire the stock at market
price? After they have control of the stock, they can pay
themselves what they think they're worth and the company
will have one, probably two, fewer people on the payroll—
the parents."

"So you think a happy ending could be a child putting financing together to acquire all the stock of the business?
John, have you been sneaking a peek at my questions? Because you're bang on—notice I didn't say dead right. Only
when a child has his or her own money in the game will they
stand back and make an honest appraisal of the business, and
more importantly an honest appraisal of their own skills at

> when a child has
> their own money in
> the game they will
> honestly appraise
> the business

making money. If kids want to proceed and invest, there are lots of books that can teach them how to raise cash for family buyouts.

"Now John I'm betting that as a manufacturer, your son, if he was given the chance, probably would have looked at your operation and wondered why, with China, India and Brazil looming as industrial powerhouses, he would want to invest in a vulnerable business. So maybe even if you had presented him with the option of buying the business he might have said no thanks. So now when you go out into the open market in an effort to sell your business to a competitor or to a financial buyer, your son can't harbor regret or anger because it was his decision to pass up owning the business. If you had given the stock to your son he might have stayed on, not because he believed in the business but because you made it easy for him to stay. Only now, his critical thinking is likely diminished—he's not looking for the risks to the business in the same way he would be if he had paid market price for the stock."

"William, do you know how good and bad that makes me feel? If what you said wasn't so simple and obvious I wouldn't be feeling like such a lousy slouch."

"Don't sell yourself short; you're a tremendous slouch. If our Family Blueprint was being reviewed each year and your son kept saying he wasn't interested in buying the stock and gaining control, do you think, as an owner, that that might be a good cue for you to start examining other options, like selling the business in whole or in part? Remember, John, doing nothing *is* a strategy, just not a really clever one." William smiled. "You know I just revealed a little more about one of the twelve questions, don't you?"

John smiled too and listened as William went on. "If and when you pursued the sale of the business, would you not want to include your son in the process now that there's a plan in place for him? After all, he has already exercised his control by saying he doesn't want to own the business and he knows there'll be upside in selling it—he'll make a pile of dough if he sticks around and actually helps sell the business for its full value. Now parent and child are on the same page and they can go about executing the plan before market forces destroy a business that neither wants to own."

"I like your logic. A Family Blueprint would have shown Michael and me that in fact there was no succession plan in place, it just looked like there was because Michael was sitting there in the corner office. If the children don't want to buy the stock and the parent doesn't have life insurance to pay the business taxes when he dies, then we have a very large bomb waiting to explode. If the family elects, like many, to do nothing, the bomb will go off, unless of course the parent lives forever."

"Well, that's a distinct possibility; I read that a hundred years old is the new ninety," William replied. "What you have described would definitely be a bad ending for our book." The waiter glided to the table to take their orders. John opted for the mahi mahi and William the grilled tuna.

John was looking a bit perplexed. "I think I see a problem. If the children want to buy the business, they want to get it at the lowest price but the parent, the seller, wants to get the highest possible price. Now child and parent aren't on the same page."

"I disagree," said William. "They are on the same page: it's called 'business' and all the family issues are background noise. It's a commercial transaction with both parties—buyer and seller—assessing their risk and potential reward if they strike a deal."

"But how can they do that?"

"Well, if they can't arrive at a fair price the process gets opened up to potential outside buyers. This option carries with it both risks and opportunities, for both parents and children. Both go into the process with their eyes wide open with no one to blame or congratulate but themselves."

"Okay, I think everyone should see how this could work. Now that we have some good endings for our book, what other major themes can we cover?"

"Well, on the flight we talked about selling the business, we talked about compensation for children in the business, we talked about exit strategies for the founder, we talked about the challenges of having more than one child or relative working in the business, we talked about firing children who aren't working out in the business and finally, we discussed stock ownership. And we agreed on the plane that it would work best if a third party managed the process, at least for the first year or two. It would need to be someone the family trusts, like their accountant. They could make updating the Family Blueprint part of their annual audit or annual meeting."

"Right," John agreed. "And it would be good if lawyers, accountants, investment advisors and anyone else could request a copy of the annual blueprint update once the process is established; you know, as evidence that the twelve questions have been answered and that there are therefore no unresolved problems. These advisors could even create the imperative for the blueprint's completion with a standard annual request letter, don't you think?"

Before William could answer, the waiter arrived with John's enormous serving of mahi mahi on a bed of arugula, accompanied by a small mountain of roasted vegetables. William's tiny serving of grilled tuna and its dollop of rice looked forlorn on the oversized plate. William looked at his tuna and then at John, who simply smiled and asked William if he was on a diet.

"Very funny," replied William. "Just pass me the bread, would you?"

After they had begun to eat, John continued. "Okay. What else is important to the process of completing the Family Blueprint?"

"Well, John, I think given the sensitivity of many of the subjects covered in our blueprint it will be important for both parties to consider bringing in a professional to help facilitate the process if a major difference of opinion ever emerges when completing the plan."

"William, remember my story about the flaky consultant?"

"I said bring in a professional. You probably didn't check her credentials very closely; didn't you clue in when she asked you to join hands around the candlelit table that she was a medium and not a management consultant?"

"Eat your tuna."

"Really," William continued, "what it boils down to is that we are exposing the fact that family businesses should be no different from other businesses. They should be governed by contracts and ethical standards and good judgment. There are lots of examples of trust in non-family businesses and that trust is usually supported by three hundred years of case law."

"William my son, we are ready to draft our blueprint and enshrine the famous twelve questions into a new doctrine for family businesses."

"John, I have been living and breathing this stuff for years. I can't tell you how excited I am to finally unleash these succession tools and wealth strategies in our book. We are going to give family businesses a new tool that will help them enter a level playing field with non-family-owned businesses. We are going to remove two impediments that destroy value. First, we are going to reveal the notion of pursuing the longevity of a business as an end unto itself, as the greatest wealth-destroying force there is, and second, we are going to get parents and children pulling in the same economic direction."

"I love it," John said. "Let's get to work."

8

The Family Blueprint

It didn't take long for William to finish his fish; he eyed John's vegetables jealously. When the waiter removed the plates and asked if they would be interested in seeing the dessert menu, William cut him off mid-sentence. "Oh yeah."

The waiter returned with dessert menus, but John had spotted a simple bowl of vanilla ice cream with chocolate sauce being delivered to a nearby table and placed his order without even opening the menu. William, on the other hand, was looking for volume. "I will have the chocolate fudge mousse cake supreme, please.

"Okay," William continued, bringing the conversation back to business. "So we've made good progress on the *process* of introducing the Family Blueprint but what about the blueprint itself? Where do you think we should begin?"

"William, I can't wait another minute. Show me the damn questions!"

"Whoa, big fella—it's not just as simple as listing the questions. We need to give our family businesses the context that I got from my father the first couple of times we went through the exercise. He gave me the objective behind each question, the logic of it, so that I could understand this was not merely an exercise loaded to his advantage. He went to great lengths to help me understand that the process was aimed at helping me find my bliss in the business. He always reinforced the idea that we all needed to find our passion, whether it lay in or outside the business. The twelve questions would drive our personal happiness, which he believed was a precondition for great business success. He emphasized the fact that the questions were aimed at building consensus between the two of us about where we wanted to take the business and where we wanted to go as individuals. The word 'team' is way overworked, as is the word 'strategic,' but a strategic team was exactly what the questions were helping to craft.

"John, I can only imagine that when my great-grandfather drafted the first question for his son, he too started at the end. He asked of his son what he asked of himself: to close his eyes and paint a mental picture of what the business looked like in five years. And that's the first of the twelve questions.

Question 1 (both parent and child)
What does our family business look like in five years?

"Now John I don't know what you were expecting. I promised you simple questions and there you have it. Now let me grab a pen and give you a couple of hypothetical answers so that you can see where the real value in these questions lies. Really, the value in all these questions isn't in the individual answers but in the connectedness of them; you'll see that when we get to the end the questions, we really will have a Family Blueprint."

"Sounds good; let's begin."

William scribbled the following:

Parent's response: I see the business sold.

Child's response: I see growing our sales ten percent each year; I see acquiring a competitor.

"So you can see that the parent and child could be on two completely different paths. Let's continue with this example. To help us do that, I'm going to reveal Questions 2 and 3. I think that after all our discussions today about control it won't surprise you that my family zeroed in on the issue of stock ownership right up front in our annual meeting. Remember, business comes down to control and control comes from holding a majority of a company's voting stock. Understanding whether the children have an interest in acquiring stock is the first step in building the plan for business. It is the foundation that the strategy for the business is built on—it gets at the central issue of whether the business will transfer its ownership to anyone in the family. So the second and third questions are closely connected:

Question 2
(both parent and child if each holds stock)
Are you interested in selling your stock? If yes, to whom?

Question 3 (child)
Are you interested in buying stock and acquiring control?

"So let's do a couple of hypothetical answers," William suggested.

Parent's Response: I wish to sell all my stock to the highest bidder.

Child's Response: I wish to purchase stock and acquire control of the company.

"William, I would say that in this example we have the potential for a highly functional relationship," John observed. "We have a seller and a potential buyer. These two can get down to the business of talking about the mechanics of the stock sale, like timing, and whether the owner will sell all the stock at once or an equal portion each year—a stock purchase schedule could easily come out of the blueprint. As well, the value of the stock could be determined with the help of an accounting firm."

"Right," William agreed. "And if a stock redemption plan proceeds and stock is being transferred to the child's hands for the first time, it is absolutely vital that they sign a shareholders' agreement. More on that later. Now John, all of this looks fairly straightforward. But for a hundred years my family has understood that even when a family member has started the process of acquiring control, the business still needs to be made available to the market for potential sale at a higher price. Anything less will destroy value. So you are probably wondering what happens if the parent— the majority shareholder—elects to sell the business to a third party at a price higher than the child is interested in or capable of paying. Remember that a seller's premium will likely come with the help of the child in the negotiations and in the earn-out or holdback phase of the deal. If the child is serious about acquiring control but the value of the stock is being determined through an open-market bid process, you can see how the child is put in a position of competing against himself. This conflict can be dealt with by arriving at a loyalty payment for the child for staying on and finding the market price for the business. If the parent fails to provide enough financial upside to the child, we can predict several outcomes. One, the child may not stay until the bid process is complete and the business is sold. Alternatively, the child may stay but remain disengaged and aloof. This was never an issue in our business because every year my father set performance goals and objectives. The possibility of any family member or employee deliberately trying to destroy value in an effort to lower the price I think would have been impossible in any business that our family has controlled over the past hundred years."

"Well, I can't argue with the logic, William. Boy, did you guys run a tight ship."

"Yes indeed. Business was never emotional, it was about following a process to build a plan and then to develop strategies and tactics around the plan to create wealth. When our business made money and we met our targets and received our bonuses, we shared our emotions: we celebrated frequently. Okay, I admit—we partied hard as a family. It was easy. When you see the rest of the questions you will understand that there was nothing left for us to say to each other about the things that get ninety-nine percent of family businesses all whipped up, nothing to say about the big three: performance, compensation and control."

"Let me go back to your example," John said thoughtfully. "It just occurred to me that if the child is or has been a shareholder for some time, his circumstances might change. The process your family followed might reveal that the child may in fact want to sell his stock back to his parents or to the corporation. That may indeed happen if the child is tired of the golden handcuffs and wants free of the stock but still likes the job. Maybe there is something Junior really wants to buy and he needs the cash."

"That's a good question. If a child answers Question 2 by expressing an interest in selling his or her stock, that speaks volumes about the direction of the succession plan, don't you think? In this scenario we have that illusion of a succession plan, nothing more. The business better get cracking on another plan."

"William, I see what's going on here with these first questions. They are showing the key players that even though a child may express no interest in owning the company he or she can still play a vital role in selling it to someone else for a premium. I can see that the key to all this is getting the parent to agree to a compensation plan for the child so that the child is genuinely excited and supportive of selling the business. I can see how this could work even if the child harbors a desire to acquire the stock and run the business himself. It's a stroke of genius. Your great-grandfather was dousing the flames of emotion with buckets of money for performance if success was achieved. Family emotion was converted into a family pulling in one direction—the direction of increasing shareholder value, ultimately through the company's sale."

"You've got it! And can you see all the interesting scenarios developing? What if the parent doesn't think much about the child's ability to run the business and doesn't think that the kid can add much value to the sale process to a third party?" William answered his own question: "The beauty of many of the twelve questions is that they force a discussion between parent and child and get to the core of the problem that plagues family businesses most: compensation. If a parent wants to keep all the sale proceeds, then our Family Blueprint will pull that information out of the parent up front. The child can govern his or her affairs accordingly and perhaps seek employment elsewhere; if that's a risk the parent wants to take then so be it…it's a business decision for everyone to consider. All of this can seem difficult and awkward but the family will be doing exactly what takes place in non-family-owned businesses. People get hired, they sign employment agreements and they cover off these precise issues. If the economic package offered isn't sufficient, the employee leaves.

"But you and I know, John, that when you add the word 'family' to the word 'business' everyone thinks hope will triumph over experience. In the event of a sale the children hope their parents will do the right thing when the time comes and compensate the kiddies fairly. Many parents do the right thing—but many don't—so out of hope may come disappointment followed by regret, followed by anger, followed by turkey dinners with many fewer people around the table."

"Again the turkey, William?"

"You'll come around, John, and see we are always talking turkey. Now don't break my stride. I'm in the zone. With a well-crafted Family Blueprint containing answers to our questions, you can see how parent and child could be high functioning because they both know exactly where the business is going and both have exercised control of their futures. No one can point fingers and say, 'Golly gosh I didn't know you were going to sell the business' or conversely, 'I didn't know you felt you were under-compensated.' Silence is the great destroyer of wealth in a family business and our questions are going to get family businesses talking. From the discussions will come quicker resolutions to simmering problems. They won't always be easy discussions, I can guarantee that, but the first safeguards for protecting family wealth will be put in place the day a Family Blueprint is born out of our questions."

> silence is the great destroyer of wealth; these questions get a family business talking

"I'll drink to that." They raised their glasses but John stopped short before they touched. William had transferred his pink umbrella to his wine glass. "William, if you think I'm going to toast a guy with a pink umbrella in his drink you're dreaming." He was only half joking.

"Fine," William said sulkily. "Let's try another set of responses to the first three questions." He picked up his pen and started to scribble, reading as he wrote. "What if the parent's response to Question 1 is, 'I see the business growing five percent each year; I see building a new facility in Texas and I see myself continuing as chairman,' and the child's response is, 'I see continuing to lead the organization, growing the organization and making it even more profitable than it already is.' And what if the parent answers no to Question 2, about whether he's interested in selling his stock, and the child answers yes to Question 3, which asks if he's interested in buying stock and acquiring control. What then?"

"I'd say it looks like we have trouble brewing on the home front, don't you think?" John told him. "It looks like the interests of the parent and child are completely misaligned."

"Not necessarily. Just imagine that the business is sailing along, posting record sales and record earnings, cash flow is fantastic and the parent is thinking, 'I could never make this kind of return on my money outside the business.' Well, there's that old saying about the calm before the storm. My point is that circumstances can change quickly in a business, and those changed circumstances can change a controlling shareholder's enthusiasm for a business."

"Well, having been a manufacturer for thirty-five years I can tell you all about the calm before the storm. I was never more nervous about the future than when sales were going well. Our sales guys would be screaming that our deliveries were falling behind and that our customers were threatening to change suppliers if we didn't improve. So late in the economic growth cycle we would find ourselves borrowing from the bank to add manufacturing capacity, which meant adding expensive buildings, adding expensive equipment... I was always worried about our debt—the amount of leverage in the business. Sure enough, I can remember three economic recessions where we got caught with too much capacity and not enough customers."

"Your example is perfect because if business conditions do indeed change over the course of the year prior to the next Family Blueprint update, this parent knows that his or her child is interested in buying the stock. Maybe the child has all the energy and optimism in the world to work through the economic slowdown. Or let's say economic conditions don't turn negative and the parent truly thinks he wants to retain control for another five years. At least in this example the child *knows* what the parent's thoughts are on the subject of stock. With the parent understanding that the child wants to acquire stock, and ultimately control, the parent may discuss a stock purchase plan that allows the child to acquire stock over a period of time longer than five years."

William's tone became gentle and he smiled. "I kept all ten versions of the answers to our questions that I completed while I was working in the family business. It's amazing the number of times we flip-flopped on the subject of selling our stock. We always reviewed the previous year's answers when we met and always had a good laugh at ourselves. Sometimes our indecision on major issues like stock ownership told us volumes: it showed us just how fragile our business was and that we should never get carried away with our own success. We must remind our readers, John, never to throw away the answers to their twelve questions. The past holds great lessons for the future. I know this—I've read my father's answers to the questions from when he worked in my grandfather's chemical company. I was able to follow their collaborative history leading to the sale of that business at the height of its value. The wealth they crystallized was reinvested into my father's insurance firm, which of course you know I ran and sold with his collaboration."

The waiter arrived with coffee and dessert. When booking the reservation William had told the head waiter that it was his friend's eightieth birthday and that he would just love it if the staff could sing "Happy Birthday." John's ice cream sported one very large candle. William's smile told John everything he needed to know. William truly enjoyed watching John squirm with embarrassment as four waiters and a busboy sang a very unharmonious rendition of "Happy Birthday," punctuating their performance with "cha cha cha" after every "happy birthday to you." When the staff dispersed, John said darkly, "You know you'll pay for that, Willy."

"Let's just get back to the blueprint. I don't want you getting any more flustered than you are." William tried to suppress his laughter. "I think in the last example, in fact in both examples we talked about, a parent/owner who wants to sell stock may elect to approach a private equity firm, for example, or competitors to buy all of the stock or assets. Now if the parent and child are working on a stock transfer plan and something starts to go fundamentally wrong with the business or in the marketplace or even with the family, the parent/owner will need to reserve the right to sell the business. We are going to assume that there is a shareholder agreement in place and that there are provisions for pulling all the shareholders along in the deal. Acquiring companies dislike dealing with minority shareholder issues. Now John, you might be amazed at how simple my family's fourth question is, but I can tell you how fundamentally important it is. William wrote it out.

Question 4 (both parent and child)
Do you understand and agree that in the interest of maximizing shareholder value this business can be sold to a third party at any time? Yes or no.

"William, this question could really set off some fireworks if the child has already expressed an interest in buying and ultimately controlling the stock of the company."

"Perhaps, but this is where my family covered off the need to follow up with special compensation for Junior—that would be me—with the fifth question; wait for it. Now let's not forget that when designing a compensation plan for Junior in the event of a sale it will be tied to Junior successfully serving what could be the most horrific year or two of his life: the holdback employment contract. And let's also not forget that the parent is going to need Junior in the negotiation phase. It is very easy for the kid to be paid some percentage of the sale proceeds that is above book value. Junior's Academy Award performance in front of the buyers will need to be convincing. The script is simple. He simply needs to convince the acquirers that if they fail to pay the high asking price and close this deal, he will take his young management team, focus and money and eat their lunch. In fact, the best thing Junior can do is look less than impressed that his money-making machine is being scooped out from under him. Buyers love to feel like winners, and if the parent is being paid lots of cash, then at least Junior must look like the loser—the loser who has to stay behind during the holdback phase. And then Junior, like all great actors, needs to be paid for his performance if he shoots the lights out.

"John, my parents and grandparents understood the importance of relying on their children to sell the business on their behalf and to pay them handsomely for their success. My family's fifth question is:

Question 5 (parent)
I agree that within the next 60 days I will put in place a special compensation formula for my child in the event that the business is sold in the next five years. Yes or no.

"John, I think we both know that this question is critical. The formula can be worked out between the parties outside the Family Blueprint; the important part is that it gets done. When it's completed, the child should be equally enthusiastic about buying the business from the parent or the parent selling it to a third party."

"I really like that the parent's and child's interests are now aligned," John enthused, "and that the two have put in place another major safeguard for preserving wealth. The parent and child can work openly and trustfully with simple goals in mind: to make money, maximize shareholder value and avert financial disaster. I can clearly see now that the love of legacy will end the moment this question is answered affirmatively."

William nodded. "This parent and child team won't make the mistake that so many other family businesses make, and that's saying, 'We will never sell the family business.' I would guess that most family businesses hold that sentiment when times have been consistently good or exceptional, when a business has consistently produced lots of earnings and nothing but good times look like they will roll forever. You and I know that buyers will typically ask to value a business based on a company's previous three years' financial performance."

"At least three, sometimes five," agreed John.

"If they want full value for their businesses, families need to be mindful of that. When a company breaks that financial winning streak they won't be realizing that full value for at least another three or four years, or longer, assuming they can get the business back on track after just one year. I think most businesses take longer than that to adjust to some major shock like a new competitor lowering prices, an economic recession, an energy crisis, a foreign exchange crisis...we could spend all night listing the things that could come out of left field and devalue a company's balance sheet."

"So most family businesses fail to understand that if they want to maximize value from their business, they need to sell before they encounter problems; after one bad year, it could take four or as long as six or seven years to convince a buyer that the problems have been fixed," John said.

"Exactly. If a family business, any business for that matter, can show consistent earnings and avoid balance sheet disasters, then real value can be realized through a sale much sooner. The sale proceeds—the wealth that has been safeguarded—can be reinvested in a variety of ways to spread the investment risk and preserve capital. Now that's a happy mission-accomplished ending."

"As I think about these questions, William, I wonder what happens if the parent wants to sell and the child doesn't want to buy?"

"That's easy, because our twelve questions will put the issues on the table for everyone to see; if the parent wants to bring in professional management or wants to hire a broker to sell the business no one can say they didn't know it was going to be sold. This entire process is helping everyone understand the distinction between compensation from employment and compensation through stock value appreciation. Remember what we talked about on the plane: with stock ownership, and certainly with ownership of the majority of stock, comes control—the control to determine when and to whom a business will be sold. If the kids decide they want to keep their great jobs in the family business but they don't want to risk their own capital to buy stock, then they better find a way of bringing in an investor who sees and understands their value to the business. That could mean finding outside funding, like a private equity investor or a bank or even a competitor, to buy some or all of the stock. The child may be able to convince this outside investor that they are key to the business and will continue to run or work in the business if an employment contract is agreed to."

"I'm really seeing now that what we're doing is formalizing the decision-making process and driving the emotion out of the relationship. The questions turn emotional subjects into basic issues that get dealt with in any other business that isn't owned and controlled by a family. These questions are so simple and obvious they seem like plain common sense."

"Yeah—so simple that you and tens of thousands of other family business owners around the world never bothered to ask them. And look at the strife and anxiety that most family businesses cause themselves as a result. Think about all the crazy family firms and all the insanity that could be avoided if someone took control and asked some of these simple questions."

"Absolutely," agreed John. "So what's next?"

"More coffee for starters....where is that waiter?" William waved to catch the waiter's attention. His caffeine levels were depleted and needed priming.

"So John. After having dealt with the issue of stock ownership, my family asked the sixth question. It is another painfully direct question, this time about unsolicited purchase offers—you know, offers that come out of the blue from competitors, private equity firms or wealthy individuals." William scribbled the question on his own notepad and slid it across the table for John to see.

Question 6 (both parent and child)
As a fundamental principle I understand that from time to time we will receive unsolicited offers from third parties to acquire the business. These offers will be considered and accepted at the discretion of the controlling shareholder and supported by the child. Yes or no.

"Now John, if a parent and child can agree on this question and also have hashed out an agreement for special compensation for family members in the event of a sale, we have a business that is positioned to succeed."

"I agree. By injecting planning into the business, we are in effect playing the 'what if' game. And these questions are getting people to keep asking 'what if' until the business is sold and control changes hands." John reviewed the questions so far. "So does that cover all the different issues related to a change in stock ownership?"

"I don't think we have enough space in our book to cover every possible scenario," William laughed, "but I positively know that the time-tested power of the first six questions will provide a good start for family businesses. The only thing I can add at this point is that families with more than one child working in the business need to decide if all the kids will answer the same questions. I would suggest that they should, because some really interesting information might be garnered by everyone involved in the process. Let's consider an example."

William sat up and prepared for his next speech. "Let's imagine that working in a family business is an elder son in a senior management position; his younger sister is in a mid-level position. Sound familiar?"

"Painfully so, William, thanks for asking."

"What if our twelve questions reveal that the son has no interest in acquiring stock and control of the business but the daughter does? What if the parent learned this for the first time? I think the possibilities are endless for businesses to learn, plan and position themselves to avoid disasters."

William got the sense that his example had brought back uncomfortable feelings for John when John said, "When do your questions turn attention to all the outside family issues that creep into a family business? You know—the problems that cause so much disruption?"

"Not so fast. We still have some housekeeping to do. Even though we have reached an agreement that the business can be shopped to, or entertain offers from, third parties, the business simply may not sell—it usually takes years to sell a business if you want to realize its full value. My great-grandfather understood this perfectly and insisted that one of the questions focus on ensuring that business owners complete a current valuation of the business annually and that they ensure there is enough insurance in place to pay the estate taxes if the controlling shareholder dies or becomes disabled. And let me say that if there are minority shareholders in the business, the right kind and the right amount of insurance is doubly critical. Can you imagine minority shareholders coming to the realization that their stock isn't worth the paper it's printed on because the founder, who died in a car crash the day before, didn't have insurance to pay the taxes?"

"Let me tell you a story," John said, "about what can happen if you don't have a valuation done. I know a family business in a town not far from where I live. The father started a pharmaceutical business, it grew successfully and the owner encouraged his two sons to join soon after they had finished college. The father wanted to transfer ownership of his business to his sons and began to have the company redeem his stock. At the same time, his sons borrowed heavily from the bank to acquire stock and ultimately control of the business. The father timed the last sale redemption to coincide with the expiration of a number of patents and royalty payments from license agreements. The sons effectively bought a business that was worth materially less than what they had paid. The sons never thought to conduct a thorough due diligence investigation on their father's business."

"John, what kind of father would put the screws to his own kids?" William shook his head. "The seventh question covers these issues."

Question 7 (parent)
In preparation for the annual update of this blueprint I will arrange for an updated valuation of the business and will calculate whether there is an appropriate amount of insurance in place. I will furnish evidence that this has been done and that estate taxes will not impair the ability of this corporation to function after my death. Yes or no.

"So William, with all the compensation issues resolved and stock ownership plans in place it looks like our parent and child team can now get down to some serious business and focus on operations, correct? What's the next issue for annual review?"

"That's easy. My family's eighth question deals with the big picture. It's one of those questions that gets everyone thinking about the forest, not the trees. The order in which this question appears is brilliant, in my opinion. It's like my great-grandfather knew that once everyone understood that the family business was for sale and everyone understood what money was to be made or lost if the business succeeded or failed, the family could finally have an honest discussion about the business itself. The first real discussion about the business's *capacity* to make money involves open talk about the strengths, weaknesses, opportunities and threats to the business."

"William—that's a SWOT analysis: strengths, weaknesses, opportunities and threats. Are you telling me your great-grandfather invented the SWOT analysis?" John was incredulous.

"Invented? No. Adopted something similar? You bet. You see? All the lessons to be learned about family business really are embedded in history. You don't need multipart spreadsheets and fancy complicated concepts that confuse people."

"I confess, William, that as popular and proven as the SWOT analysis is, I never completed one with my son or daughter. I mean, how could we when the big issues, like selling the business, were deemed completely out of bounds for discussion. Honestly, how could I have ever had a discussion with Michael about the threats to the business and come up with a big long list of issues that could kneecap us when I knew I couldn't continue the discussion to its logical conclusion, which was 'Let's sell.' "

"Exactly." William scribbled the eighth question so fast John could barely read his writing.

Question 8 (both parent and child)
List at least three items in each of the following four categories that could affect the health of the business over the next five years: strengths, weaknesses, opportunities and threats.

John noted, "Here, too, I don't think we want people writing big long essays. We want very focused and precise answers. Let me give you some examples of the kind of answers I think we're looking for."

Strengths	1. High product quality
	2. Good brand loyalty
	3. Strong sales growth potential
Weaknesses	1. Lots of debt
	2. Running at full capacity
	3. Old management style
Opportunities	1. License our technology
	2. Develop new products
	3. One competitor in disarray
Threats	1. Bigger, better-funded competitors with global reach
	2. Rising raw-material costs, poor purchasing power
	3. Located in high-cost country; threats from cheap imports

"With our individual lists complete, my father and I would sit down and try to compile a single list of strengths, weaknesses, opportunities and threats that we agreed on. When that list was complete we were ready for the next question, which is a very focused question and one that brought the shelf life of our business into clear focus. The question is really a vote of confidence for whatever we decided together were the strengths, weaknesses, opportunities and threats facing our company.

"The ninth question helps clarify whether a family business is at the beginning, middle or end of its life cycle."

Question 9 (both parent and child)
To secure our future prosperity together we should either:

A. Continue to run our business and invest more of our money in our company. Yes or no.

OR

B. Proactively pursue the sale of our company. Yes or no.

"Wow, William," John said, impressed. "Your family sure knew how to pick 'em!"

"Well, I guess our family's collective history tells us that a business is either growing or it's shrinking. I don't know too many businesses that successfully stay the same size for very long."

"Oh, I agree. And hey—this fits right into my theory about everything having a beginning, a middle and an end," John added, pleased with himself.

"Yes indeed," William confirmed. "But I think it's very hard for founders to see the end. Their business is their identity and they lose sight of the fact that a business is simply an instrument of wealth creation. For many, the end of their business brings their own mortality into focus. If the business is alive then the founder is alive. It takes great insight and self-awareness to write your own corporate obituary; few have the capacity to sell at the top of their game."

"That was beautiful. You could be a literary giant."

"Thank you, thank you very much," replied William.

John could not decide whether William had actually tried to sound like Elvis. "You know, William, I am reminded of a town not far from where I live that every four years, prior to the local elections, debates whether it should allow more development or stop growing. I am amazed that there are people who actually believe that you can keep a town the exact same size forever. Towns, like businesses, are either getting bigger or getting smaller. You can slow growth and accelerate growth, just like you can slow contraction or accelerate it. I just don't think you can make keeping something the same size a realistic goal. I think it's delusional."

"Delusional? Are you suggesting we need a question that probes the founder's mental health?"

"Having been called senile and crazy by various members of my family on the same day, I'm a little sensitive on this topic, but I digress. I'm hoping that one of your remaining questions forces the founder to examine his personal wealth strategy. We need something that gets the parent/founder to assess how much appetite he or she has for continuing to risk new money."

"John, I'm impressed. But new money is kind of like old money—no one wants to lose any of it. If the parent has answered yes to Question 9(A), then the parent is probably still very much engaged in the business and feels confident about the future...his future. After all, his future is the company's future; he owns the majority of the stock. If the parent answers no to Question 9(A) but yes to Question 9(B), then both parent and child will understand that they had better be talking about the sale of the company or a stock redemption plan sooner rather than later—assuming, of course, that the child is interested. Not too many businesses can operate profitably without a commitment to new investment by the owners. If nothing else, Question 9 will get parent and child thinking about proactively pursuing the sale of the business right away."

"So essentially," John said, "it's better to get on with it than to wait for the company's financial health to deteriorate. Every business that's for sale needs a story and a good story needs time to build. The sooner a family business can get its story built, the more an acquirer will pay for the business. If a buyer senses randomness or desperation in a family business, they will mop the floor with you."

"You say that like you have personal experience."

"Thanks for reminding me."

"Okay. So, we've arrived at the tenth question. It deals with one of the biggest, if not *the* biggest, issue that destroys family businesses. By the time families get to this question they should have developed a good understanding of the health and future of their company and they should all clearly understand that compensation for work performed is separate from stock ownership."

"But," John interrupted, "they also need to understand that it is normal for salary to be determined by industry standards. Most accounting firms and industry associations can provide guidance on what similar firms pay individuals for various positions. In addition to salary, performance bonuses come in many shapes and sizes and can be tied to individual goals and objectives and to overall corporate performance metrics. It's important to remember that when you pay relatives working in the business what they're worth—pay them fairly for the value they add—other relatives, both inside and outside the business, have nothing to be jealous of."

"You're absolutely right: compensation can be a technical issue and it's worth spending the time and resources to get it right, especially for a family business. An independent third party's recommendation can silence a lot of criticism by other family members. And Question 10 deals with just that."

Question 10 (parent)
Within 60 days of completing this blueprint we will complete a salary and bonus compensation review for my child.
Yes or no.

"There are still a couple of major subjects that need addressing and they're two of the biggest bombs ticking away in family businesses. My family's eleventh question defuses one of these bombs with grace and simplicity. Remember we talked about silence being the major killer of most family businesses? Our Family Blueprint needs to formalize performance feedback between parent and child. Even if the child does not report directly to the parent, there needs to be some feedback, at least annually. As I mentioned earlier, my first couple of 'question' meetings were painful. Then something changed; as I grew more confident in my role as president, the annual meeting with my father became a day I cherished. And on that day, Question 11 became my favorite.

"As a son working in my father's business, I can tell you that the owner's view of the child—the parent's view of the child—is a potent and often ignored force within a business. John, one of the reasons family businesses can be so financially successful is the unwavering commitment of a child to work excessive hours and drive success, in some cases at the expense of everything else. Often these children are paid less than market rates but achieve success that no outside manager could achieve. I am convinced that my great-grandfather understood that children working in the family's business were working for all sorts of intangible rewards: parental acknowledgment, legacy, pride, tradition…you know, all the things you can't feed your family with. I believe in my heart that he wrote his eleventh question for all the children working in family businesses."

"If I'm interpreting correctly, your great-grandfather knew that it might be fine for a child to work without any feedback or comment from the parent for a period of time but that over the medium or long term, resentment will build and the child will either quit or lose interest in the business."

"Precisely. If the parents have a stock transfer plan in mind, they may just be killing their own succession plan by leaving the child in a performance vacuum."

"And performance reviews are absolutely standard in most businesses not owned by families. They are done for a reason: people want to know that they are succeeding; it's a basic human condition. If they are succeeding they feel good, they feel a strong sense of self-worth and they give more of themselves."

"You bet. I mean, even if a child in a family business is looking at the numbers and sees that they are performing well, they need to hear it from the boss—their parent. Parents who have spent a lifetime 'toughening up' their children by withholding positive feedback may want to rethink this approach because most children will quit or refuse to acquire stock of a business in which they feel like failures. Trust me on this one, John; never being good enough gets old real fast…especially when the child is actually an adult. So to avoid all of this acrimony, we have my family's eleventh question.

Question 11 (parent)
I agree to conduct an annual performance review of my child. This review will measure performance against mutually agreed on and achievable goals and objectives. New goals and objectives will be set for the coming year. Yes or no.

"John, somehow in our book we must get across to our readers that a parent's failure to give regular feedback to a child is bad for business and bad for the relationship. And it can lead to the rapid and irreversible destruction of wealth."

"I agree it's bad for business, but let's imagine that the child is a poor performer, in over their head. That will come out in the performance review," John said with concern.

"And that's a good thing," said William. "We agreed on the plane that a family business isn't a charity; it's not some convenient mechanism for dispensing wealth to needy incompetent children. A family business that allows that kind of thing to take place drives good employees to find alternative employment. A parent/owner can't have two conflicting employment performance standards in place and expect to run a sustainable business—the wealth-destruction process is well underway in businesses where that is allowed to happen and its effects will be swift and the damage permanent. I bet we can both think of families that view their businesses as ATMs. But can you imagine the awkwardness that a non-family vice president of finance or a controller feels when he or she sees chronically underperforming relatives in the business running personal expenses through the business, in some cases without the knowledge of the owner?"

"That would not be good," replied John.

"No, it would not. The annual performance review can be the most important meeting between relatives in a business. If it's conducted positively, everyone can emerge with clarity and confidence about their roles. There are many resources available to help owners who have never conducted a formal performance review. Many experts believe that a good review involves the employee doing eighty percent of the talking— about their experience over the past year and what they want to accomplish in the coming year. Great reviewers are superb listeners. Nowhere is listening more important than in family businesses, right? Nowhere is talking more important than in a family business."

"I find that you're a good listener, William."

"Thank you," said William. "And on that note, did I hear you say something about me picking up the tab for dinner?"

"Sorry to disappoint, buddy, but the waiter would never stick the birthday boy with the tab. I told you you would pay. With your fancy PhD I figured you'd be more strategic."

William looked at John blankly, realizing he'd outsmarted himself. "John, I can see why you were so successful at building a $100 million business."

John laughed at having trumped William.

"So getting back to business," William said overly firmly, "the last question deals with a topic that we spent a great deal of time on today, something we just touched on—sibling rivalry."

"I was wondering when we were going to get some clarity on the rules of engagement for more than one child or relative working in a business. Having had my daughter *and* my son working in the business at one point I know the importance of this subject."

"I think most kids roam through a family business like it was their own sandbox. They take too much latitude on everything and this inevitably causes problems between children and between employees who are loyal to each child or relative in the business. Again, when we look to non-family enterprises for guidance, we see the use of job descriptions to clearly define what it is that people should be doing, the scope of their responsibilities and who they will report to. An organizational chart is usually attached to the job description. I know lots of companies that carry out performance reviews and have job descriptions for everyone *but* the relatives in the business. It's as if the owner believes the process of family reviewing family is too much to bear, too much for the reviewer and the reviewee. We already talked about how sensitive family members are to criticism or perceived criticism, so we need to offer a word of caution in our book to parents that the review of their children needs to be approached like the nuclear bomb that it feels like. I would think a hundred positive comments to one constructive, delicately phrased performance recommendation would be about the right ratio.

"So we solve these problems with Question 11 and with our final question." William jotted the last question down and turned the notepad for John to read.

Question 12 (parent)
Within 60 days of completing this blueprint I will present up-to-date job descriptions to all family members working in the business that clearly describe their duties and responsibilities. I will include an up-to-date organizational chart. Family members working in the company will adhere to the company's policies and procedures. Yes or no.

"So you can see, John, even if the parent is out of the day-to-day operations of the business but is still the controlling share-holder, they absolutely need to update the Family Blueprint each year. This point is absolutely critical. The chairman/owner or non-executive chairman or whatever he wants to call himself cannot abdicate his responsibility to manage his family members' performance in the business. Using job descriptions and annual performance reviews is absolutely necessary regardless of the size of business—even if the child is the only employee. Everyone needs to clearly understand what's expected of them; everyone needs to know whether they're succeeding; it's human nature. I think we agree that failure to do this is shortening the fuse on a rather large bomb that will detonate when the parent least expects it."

"I completely agree," John said, "and I'm not saying that just because you agreed to pick up the tab for dinner. When this process isn't carried out, family members will view the parent/owner as disengaged, indifferent and out of touch. And when that happens, anarchy, disrespect for company values and a veritable free for all among family members follows, destroying the business from the inside out." John realized a connection. "That would be the China Syndrome you mentioned earlier."

William smiled. "Yes. And conversely, a properly managed family business, even with multiple family members involved, can thrive with each child or relative striving to meet their own individual and corporate goals and objectives. I'm feeling good about our Family Blueprint," William said with satisfaction. "The twelve questions it contains cut right to the performance issues, the compensation issues and the control issues. These simple questions get parents and children to peer into the future together and ask 'what if.'

"I think all businesses have a childlike quality about them: they are organic and human, full of potential, always changing and always requiring attention, money, time and patience. Family businesses have an extra layer of complexity, a layer of family love, an extra component that gives them advantages and disadvantages over non-family-owned competitors."

"Yes," William agreed, nodding vigorously, "and so we have to make sure that the families running these businesses take care of themselves. We both know from our own experience that there is so much love and goodwill and enthusiasm when children start in their parents' businesses. They have been offered an opportunity to grow and learn, an opportunity they might not have had if they had pursued careers outside the business. We also know that these extraordinary feelings of trust and love can fray and deteriorate into something so soul-destroying that no amount of money can buy solace, repair the broken dreams or cure the pain caused by individuals moving through a family business in different directions, with different expectations."

"I think the greatest contribution we can make with our book, William, is the relief we will provide to families when they hear that it's okay to mix family and business, that it's simply unrealistic for a parent and child to pretend they aren't related when they discuss business issues. No wonder so many families feel like failures in their own businesses. They have been set up to fail from the start. No wonder only three percent make it to the third generation—what is being asked of them is unnatural, impractical and simply wrong."

"So we can acknowledge that families are complex, that they are loaded with passion. And what's wrong with passion—it's what makes these businesses tick. Can you imagine a more powerful wealth-creating machine than a business full of hard-working, trusting, passionate individuals? Take the gas station owned by that couple on the plane and put it beside a non-family-owned station and I'll tell you which one I would invest in. In the family-owned gas station we have labor that is flexible, labor that has pride of ownership, a business that can capitalize and fund itself quickly without bureaucracy. We have one of the most powerful economic forces on the planet. We can help this wealth-generating machine take better care of itself, help it preserve its natural advantage, by giving it a simple planning tool with which, once a year, family members can plug their noses and dive into critical performance, compensation and control issues. They will emerge with clarity about where they're going together as a family and together as a business. They can remove the wondering from the business and replace it with planning based on the very trust and love from which the business was born."

"William, maybe the annual Family Blueprint meeting will be a time when the love flows in the business, when the children hear from their parents what a terrific job they're doing and how proud their parents are of them. They can celebrate what they've built together. You've convinced me: you can't take the family out of a family business, and I think people who believe they can have utterly missed the boat. Family love mismanaged, misjudged, exploited and most of all ignored will destroy wealth and families faster than any economic force."

"John," William said as he gathered his papers, "our work is done for the evening. May I say what a pleasure it has been dining with you and creating something so vastly more important than anything I ever accomplished in the insurance business?"

"Not so fast. What you did with your father in your business shaped your experience and views of family business; I'd say that's pretty important. In a way, your father helped shape our book. I'd like to meet him some day. The nut doesn't fall far from the tree, and I suspect he is a very special man who gave his children lots of freedom to explore their full potential. I confess my jealousy of the relationship you forged with him and of the way you both used your trust and love to accomplish great commercial success—and great family success."

"Thank you. That means a lot coming from you."

As the two left the restaurant, John said, "What do you say we grab a nightcap at the bar and talk about something completely unrelated to family businesses? You a sports fan, William?"

"Yeah, I'm a big Yankees fan—now there's an interesting family business…"

Readers

You Can Join The Conversation

Visit

www.EveryFamilysBusiness.com

Click on Reader Comments and
share your thoughts about this book.

Postscript

In the more than 500 convention speeches I have delivered since *Every Family's Business* was first published in February 2008, one sentence always elicits an uneasy, awkward laugh from the audience: "In this room there are children who believe their parents will gift their business to them, and parents who believe their children will purchase their business." I believe this singular issue—this lack of clarity over the future ownership of the business—is the greatest source of conflict and wealth destruction in a business.

Only when business owners truly understand how temporary, fragile and fleeting a business is can they take the first step to invest in the only real thing that can be sustained, the only thing that can produce a legacy: their family. This investment in family means avoiding the temptation of gifting an operating business to the ones you love.

History teaches us in excruciating detail that if you ignore this advice, your "gift" will elicit the total opposite of your intended result. Instead, make a gift of your wealth, give your wealth of experience, give your entrepreneurial wisdom, give opportunity—and watch your real legacy take flight.

It is hard for business owners to contemplate and plan their last deal. I hope *Every Family's Business* gives you a new practical tool to help you find the end of your business before the end finds you. And when you do, celebrate the idea that the best is yet to come—and that it has both everything and nothing to do with you.

Tom Deans
Hockley Valley

Public Speaking

One of the least expected but most rewarding experiences in writing this book has been the opportunity to travel extensively and speak to business owners and their families about the personal experiences that led me to write *Every Family's Business*.

Most of my speeches have been organized by accountants, wealth management professionals, financial services firms, merger and acquisition firms, industry associations and family offices. If you own a business, or advise business owners, and want to learn more about booking Tom Deans, please contact **info@EveryFamilysBusiness.com**.

A portion of my speaking fee will be donated to a charity in the area that supports youth entrepreneurship.

The Long Awaited Sequel

Willing Wisdom:
7 Questions Successful Families Ask

When William parlays his international best-selling book on family businesses into a career as a professional speaker, he is confronted with a new set of challenging questions. None more complex than how families should divide their estates. *Willing Wisdom* sets out to help families talk about money and aging. If you enjoyed *Every Family's Business*, you're going to thoroughly enjoy this new critically acclaimed best-selling sequel.

You can order your copy of *Willing Wisdom* by visiting www.WillingWisdom.com and receive free express shipping. Books ship on the same day orders are received and usually arrive in 2-5 business days. Alternatively, you can complete the order form at the back of this book and fax to 519-938-5407 or send an email to sales@WillingWisdom.com.

Notes

Notes

Notes

_____

_____

_____

_____

_____

_____

_____

_____

_____

_____

_____

_____

_____

_____

Order More Copies of

Every Family's Business

"A Gift That Says Family Is Important"

FREE EXPRESS SHIPPING

Fax Completed Form to: 519-938-5407

Name: _____

Address: _____

City: _____ State/Province: _____

Zip/Postal Code: _____ Phone: _____

Email: _____

Ship to (if different from above):

Name: _____

Address: _____

City: _____ State/Province: _____

Zip/Postal Code: _____ Phone: _____

Email: _____

Quantity ordered: _____ × $22.95* = _____

*Plus applicable taxes. Books ship FREE the same day that orders are received and typically arrive within to 2 to 5 business days.

Credit card type: Visa _____ MasterCard _____

Credit card #: _____

Expiry date: _____

Name on card: _____

Signature for Credit Card: _____

Order The Sequel

Willing Wisdom

FREE EXPRESS SHIPPING
Fax Completed Form to: 519-938-5407

Name: _____

Address: _____

City: _____ State/Province: _____

Zip/Postal Code: _____ Phone: _____

Email: _____

Ship to (if different from above):

Name: _____

Address: _____

City: _____ State/Province: _____

Zip/Postal Code: _____ Phone: _____

Email: _____

Quantity ordered: _____ × $22.95* = _____

*Plus applicable taxes. Books ship FREE the same day that orders are received and typically arrive within to 2 to 5 business days.

Credit card type: Visa _____ MasterCard _____

Credit card #: _____

Expiry date: _____

Name on card: _____

Signature for Credit Card: _____